Use White Space

Layout—how you arrange material on a page or screen—determines whether your correspondence is readable. Essentially, avoid dense blocks of prose, overly cluttered pages, or largely empty pages.

Q How should I use white space?

To balance dark print, build white space into your page layout. (You can do so for both print and electronic documents.) Used well, white space rests readers' eyes, "chunks" related information, and highlights key ideas and details. Follow these guidelines:

Use healthy margins. Frame your page with generous margins, generally 1" or 1½" on all sides of a standard 8½" x 11" sheet. Adjust margins to account for the type of page (e.g., a brochure vs. a memo).

Break up text. Use techniques like these to keep your prose from getting heavy and dense on the page:

- Double-space between paragraphs and keep paragraphs short.
- Surround headings with white space—generally, more space above than below the heading.
- Turn some material into lists (see page **84**).
- Increase line spacing to 1.5 or 2, if necessary.

FYI Avoid **too much white space**. In some documents, an imbalance of white space over black print can suggest thin content.

Ineffective   **Effective**

Vary Typography

Use typographical techniques that make your document attractive and draw attention to key points. Pay attention, in particular, to type size and style.

Q How should I use different type sizes?

When selecting type size, consider reading conditions and the impact needed.

- **For normal reading conditions**, make main text 10 or 12 points.
- **For impact** in titles, headings, subheadings, and key selling points, increase size 2–4 points. Make the jump noticeable but not drastic.
- **For presentations**, think big: 18–36 points. Consider the people in the back row.

Main text	10–12
Subheading	14
Heading	16
Title	18
Presentation	18–36

Q How should I use different typestyles?

When using typestyle for a special effect, follow these simple guidelines:

- **Be thoughtful:** Use each stylistic effect with intent, not for dazzle.
- **Be frugal:** Avoid combining several techniques.
- **Be distinctive:** Use effects to set off special text from normal text.

UPPERCASE	Uppercase is more prominent than lowercase but harder to read in extended passages.
Underlining	Underlining is useful for indicating subheadings, key words, and key sentences, but avoid using it for extended passages.
Highlighting	Highlighting and similar techniques such as shading and outlining draw attention to key words and statements.
Boldface	Boldface causes print to jump out. It's especially useful for headings, subheadings, warnings, and other key information.
Italics	Italics indicates book titles, words designated as words, and key statements. Avoid it, however, for extended passages because it is difficult to read.
Color	Color helps highlight headings, warnings, tips, and other key material. However, make sure that color combinations work well.

Use Color to Strengthen the Message

For most correspondence, black and white is fine—flexible, conservative, and cost effective. However, color can effectively get your reader's attention and communicate your message, especially in sales literature.

Q How should I use color?

1. **Consider using color in four places.**
   - **Paper:** Colored paper attracts attention, but choose wisely: subtle, traditional colors (like tan, blue, or green) imply strength and stability; pastels, lightness; neon colors, advertising.
   - **The Computer Screen:** For word processing software and e-mail programs, an off-white background works best. However, Web pages and presentation software use brighter and deeper colors to attract attention. Caution: generally avoid a black background.
   - **Graphics:** Graphs, charts, photographs, and drawings—colorful graphics can powerfully enhance your correspondence.
   - **Text and Background:** Vary from the standard black on a neutral background to create emphasis in headings, boxes, menus, lists, and so on. You can vary the text color, the background color, or both.

2. **Use colors to feature material.** Draw the reader's attention to key elements such as headings, bullets, text boxes, visuals, and special statements.

3. **Use colors attractively.** First, limit your color palette. Avoid a confusing look, clashing colors (e.g., green and orange), and colors that are hard on the eyes. Don't overdo color features; instead, consider both color unity and variety for the document as a whole. Second, stress or soften features with your color combinations. For example, black and yellow or red and white "pop," whereas blue and ivory create a soft, subtle effect.

Index

Abbreviations,
   U.S. Postal, 40
Accusatory language, 50
Active voice, 96
Address,
   E-mail, 17
   Envelope, 39
   Forms of, 34–37
   Inside, 28, 30
   Titles in, 34–37
Agreement,
   Pronoun-antecedent, 98
   Subject-verb, 100
AIDA, 44, 78

AMBIGUOUS wording, 98–99
   Dangling modifiers, 99
   Indefinite pronoun reference, 98
   Misplaced modifiers, 99
   Unclear wording, 98

Analyze, 16, 20, 52, 60
Announcement,
   Negative, 43
Antecedent, pronoun agreement, 98
Apology, 62
Application letter, 26
Application-related documents, 26
Attachments,
   E-mail, 16
   Memo, 22, 23
Attention line, 30

BAD-NEWS messages, 43
   Bid rejection, 64
   Claim denial, 65
   Crisis management, 43
   Guidelines, 26, 43
   Negative announcement, 43

BEBE, 43
Bid form, sales proposal, 73
Bid rejection, 64
Business English, 92

Chart,
   Type of correspondence, 7
CHECKLISTS,
   Customer-service letters, 66
   Sales letters, 58
   Sales proposals, 74

Claim denial, 65
Claims,
   Of policy, 78
   Of truth, 78
   Of value, 78
   Support of, 79
Cliché, 91
Closing,
   Complimentary, 28
   Letter, 29, 53, 54, 55
   Memo, 21
Collective nouns, 100
Color,
   Use of, 103, 104
Comparisons, creative, 80
Complimentary closing, 28
Compound subject, 100
Confidential notation, 22, 24, 30
Conjunction,
   Coordinating, 94
   Subordinating, 94
Continuation pages, 30
Coordinating conjunctions, 94
Copies notation, 22, 30
   Letter, 30
   Memo, 22
Copy, correct, writing trait, 97–100
Correct copy, 97–100
Correspondence,
   Parts of, 4–5
   Real-time, 11–18
   Strengthening, seven traits of, 77–104
   Written, 8
Courtesy titles, 34–37
Cover sheet, fax, 24
Credit application,
   Approval of, 42
Crisis management memo, 43

Customer-service letters, 59–66
   Bid rejection, 64
   Checklist, 66
   Claim denial, 65
   Guidelines, 60
   Invitation, 61
   Positive adjustment, 62
   Positive reply to an inquiry, 63

D

Dangling modifiers, 99
Dates on letters, 28
Denials, claims, 65
Design, document,
   Basic design principles, 101–104
Design, effective, writing trait, 101–104
Double negative, 97
Double preposition, 97
Double subject, 97
Drafting, 16, 20, 27, 52, 60, 68

Effective writing, seven traits of, 77–104
   Correct copy, 97–100
   Effective Design, 101–104
   Logical organization, 81–84
   Precise words, 89–92
   Professional voice, 85–88
   Smooth sentences, 93–96
   Strong ideas, 78–80
Electronic résumé, follow-up, 26

E-MAIL, 16–18
   Basic model, 17
   Credit approval, 42
   Etiquette, 12, 13
   Flame wars (arguments), 18
   Guidelines, 16
   Thank you, 72
   When to use, 7

Emoticons, 13, 18
Enclosures,
   Letter, 28
   Memo, 22

Envelope guidelines, 38, 39
Ethics, e-mail, 18
Etiquette,
  E-mail, 12, 13
  Cell phone, 12, 13
  Instant messaging, 12, 13
Expanded letter, 30–31
Expanded memo, 22–23

Faxes,
  Format, 24
  Model, 24
Flaming, 18
Flowery phrase, 91
Folding letters, 38
Formal tone, 88
Formats,
  Business letter, 28
  Design, 32
  Full-block, 32, 33
  Letter, 32
  Memo, 22
  Semiblock, 32, 33
  Simplified, 32, 33

FORMS OF ADDRESS,
  Courtesy titles, 34–37
  Gender-specific, 35
  Official titles, 36
  Professional titles, 34
  Religious titles, 37

Full-block letter format, 32–33

Gender, titles, 35

GOOD-NEWS and neutral messages, 42
  Apology, 62
  Cover sheet, fax, 24
  Credit approval, 42
  Guidelines, 42
  Information request, 15
  Invitation, 61
  Positive adjustment, 62
  Positive reply to an inquiry, 63
  Thank-you message, 72

Government titles, 36
Graphics, 103, 104
GUIDELINES,
  Bad-news messages, 43
  Designing graphics, 103
  E-mail messages, 16
  Good-news and neutral messages, 42
  Letters, 27
  Memos, 20
  Proposals, 68–69
  Sales letters, 52

Heading,
  Informative, 81
  Letter, 28, 29
  Memo, 21, 22

Ideas, strong, writing trait, 78–80
Identification line, 30
Indefinite pronouns, 100
Informal tone, 88
Information request, 15
Initialisms, 13
Inquiry reply, 29, 31, 63
Inside address, 28, 30
Instant messaging, 13
  Successful, 15
  Using, 14
  Writing, 15
International mail, 39
Invitation, 61

Jargon, 88–90

Language,
  Accusatory, 50
  Business English, 92
  Gender, 35
  Nonstandard, 97
Legal notices, 26

LETTERS, 25–40
  Application, 26
  Appreciation, 26
  Basic letter, parts of,
    Guidelines, 28
    Model, 29
  Customer-service, 59–66
  Envelope guidelines, U.S. Postal Service (USPS), 39–40
    International mail, 39
    Standard abbreviations, 40
    When to use, 7, 26
  Expanded letter,
    Guidelines, 30
    Model, 31
    Reference line, 30
  Folding, 38
  Guidelines, writing, 27
  Letter formats, 28, 30, 32
    Models, 29, 31, 33
  Professional appearance, 101–104
    Paper, 104
  Sales, 51–58

Lists,
  Numbered, 84
  Presentation, 84

MEMOS, 19–23
  Attachment, 22, 23
  Basic, 21
  Closing, 21, 22
  Confidential, 22, 23
  Creating effective, 20
  Expanded, 22, 23
  Format, 21, 22
  Guidelines, writing, 20
  Heading, 21–23
  Initials, 21–23
  Models, 21, 23
  When to use, 7

Business and Sales Correspondence
Trait-Based Strategies That Improve Writing and Save Time

Verne Meyer ■ Pat Sebranek ■ John Van Rys

Acknowledgements

Editorial Director: Patrick Sebranek
Director of Marketing: Thomas Spicuzza
Cover Design: Chris Krenzke and Colleen Belmont
Illustrations: Chris Krenzke
Project Manager: Steve Augustyn
Editorial: Rob King, Lois Krenzke
Design and Production: Colleen Belmont, Tammy Hintz, Kathy Strom, Kevin Nelson, Chris Krenzke

Copyright © UpWrite Press 2008. All Rights Reserved.

No part of this book may be reproduced or transmitted in any form or by any means, electronic or mechanical, including photocopying and recording, or by any information storage or retrieval system without the prior written permission of UpWrite Press unless such copying is expressly permitted by federal copyright law. Address inquiries to UpWrite Press, 35115 West State Street, Burlington, WI 53105. (All other trademarks are the property of their respective owners.)

1 2 3 4 5 6 7 8 9 10 -FRZ- 11 10 09 08 07

ISBN 978-1-932436-24-2
Printed in Canada

Contents

Section 1
Understanding Correspondence 1

1 Planning Successful Correspondence 3
Parts of Correspondence 4
Getting Started 6
Choosing the Best Medium 7
Best Practices 8

Section 2
Writing Correspondence 9

2 Creating Real-Time Correspondence 11
Real-Time Correspondence Etiquette 12
Instant Messaging at Work 14
Anatomy of a Successful Instant Message 15
Guidelines for E-Mail 16
Basic E-Mail 17
Curing "Flame Wars" 18

3 Writing Memos and Faxes 19
Guidelines for Memos 20
Basic Memo 21
Expanded Memo Format 22
Expanded Memo 23
Fax Cover Sheet 24

4 Writing Business Letters 25
Top Ten Times to Write a Letter 26
Guidelines for Letters 27
Basic Letter Format 28
Basic Letter 29
Expanded Letter Format 30
Expanded Letter 31
Full-Block, Semiblock, and Simplified Letters 32
Forms of Address 34
Folding Letters 38
Addressing Envelopes 39
Standard Abbreviations 40

5 Organizing with Purpose 41
Good and Neutral News (SEA) 42
Bad-News Messages (BEBE) 43
Persuasive Messages (AIDA) 44

6 Writing Sales Correspondence 45
Targeting the Reader's Needs 46
Making a Claim 46
Testing and Supporting a Claim 47
Tailoring Support to the Reader 48
Addressing Competing Claims 49
Winning the Reader's Trust 50

7 **Writing Sales Letters 51**
   Guidelines for Sales Letters 52
   Form Sales Letter 53
   Targeted Sales Letter 54
   Sales Letter Following a Contact 55
   Sales Letter Following a Sale 56
   Sales Letter to an Inactive Customer 57
   Checklist for Sales Letters 58

8 **Writing Customer-Service Letters 59**
   Guidelines for Customer-Service Letters 60
   Invitation 61
   Positive Adjustment 62
   Positive Reply to an Inquiry 63
   Bid Rejection 64
   Claim Denial 65
   Checklist for Customer-Service Letters 66

9 **Writing Sales Proposals 67**
   Guidelines for Sales Proposals 68
   Unsolicited Sales Proposal 70
   RFP for a Small Project 71
   Sales Proposal Follow-Up E-Mail 72
   Solicited Bid 73
   Checklist for Sales Proposals 74

Section 3
Benchmarking Your Writing with the Seven Traits 75

10 **Strengthening Seven Traits of Your Correspondence 77**
   Trait 1: Strong Ideas 78
   Trait 2: Logical Organization 81
   Trait 3: Professional Voice 85
   Trait 4: Precise Words 89
   Trait 5: Smooth Sentences 93
   Trait 6: Correct Copy 97
   Trait 7: Effective Design 101

Index 105

Section 1
Understanding Correspondence

In This Section

This section introduces you to the basics of business correspondence:

- **Parts of Correspondence 4**
- **Getting Started 6**
- **Choosing the Best Medium 7**
- **Best Practices 8**

1 Planning Successful Correspondence

No business can succeed without effective correspondence. Whether you produce, market, sell, or maintain a product or service, you need to communicate with people both inside and outside your organization.

Professional e-mails, memos, and letters elicit positive exchanges and build trust between you and colleagues, suppliers, and customers. This chapter outlines the best practices for your business correspondence—now and in the future.

Your Goal

Understand the basics of business correspondence.

- Understand the process of corresponding.
- Analyze each situation.
- Select the best medium for your message.
- Learn when to write, what to write, and how to write.

Q What are the parts of correspondence?

All correspondence includes the following parts:

- Sender
- Message
- Medium
- Receiver
- Response
- Context

When any part does not work correctly, the flow of communication gets blocked, resulting in miscommunication rather than a positive, productive exchange.

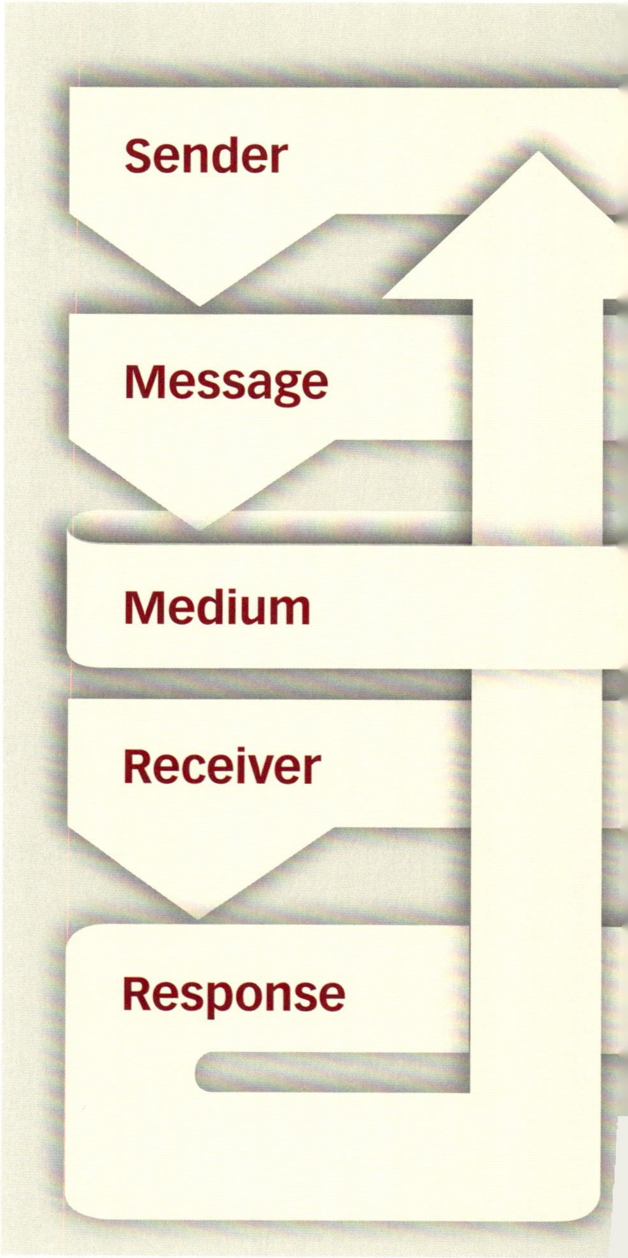

Sender

Message

Medium

Receiver

Response

The sender must understand the message, the receiver, and the context and choose the best medium for the situation.

The message must present clear ideas, logical organization, a professional voice, strong words, smooth sentences, correct grammar, and a reader-friendly design.

The medium (e-mail, memo, IM, or letter) must have the right formality, speed, capacity, and reliability.

The receiver must "decode" the message, understand it, and consider how to act on it.

The response (feedback, follow-up, action) must be correct, clear, compelling, and timely.

Context

All the variables must function within the larger context of the organization, its mission, and the issue presented in the message.

Business and Sales Correspondence

Q How can I get started?

Begin by analyzing the situation. Think about the goal of your message, the needs of the receiver, and the overall context. The following worksheet shows the kinds of questions you can ask yourself as you begin to write a correspondence.

Situation Analysis Worksheet

Message Goal
1. What do I want the receiver to **know**? _____
2. What do I want the receiver to **do**? _____
3. What **realistic, measurable outcome** do I want? _____

Receiver
1. What are the receiver's
    values? _____
    needs? _____
    problems? _____
    priorities? _____
2. How will the receiver **benefit** from my message? _____
3. How **knowledgeable** about the issue is the receiver? _____
4. How **resistant** will the receiver be to the message? _____
5. What **relationship** do we have? _____

Context
1. Is the document **internal** or **external**? _____
2. Is the document **solicited** or **unsolicited**? _____
3. What **medium** should I use? _____
4. **When** should the message arrive? _____
5. What **other factors** affect the situation? _____

How can I choose the best medium?

Consider where the medium falls on the continuum of communication:

Continuum Of Communication					
Casual, Quick, Personal ←———————————————→ **Formal, Slow, Corporate**					
Face to Face	Phone	Instant Message	E-Mail	Memo	Letter

Communication on the left side of the continuum is rich in contextual cues, such as facial expression and tone of voice. Communication on the right side has very few contextual cues. Choose the medium that will most likely achieve the goal of your message.

When should I use written correspondence?

Though much business communication can be handled orally (face to face or on the phone), written correspondence should be used if . . .

- the message is **complicated**.
- the message is **formal**.
- the message requires **documentation**.
- you have a large **audience**.

For especially important communication, use both oral and written communication (e.g., a conference call followed up by meeting minutes).

Should I write an e-mail, a memo, or a letter?

Consult this chart to decide which type of correspondence to use:

Write e-mail for . . .	Write memos for . . .	Write letters for . . .
routine business speed wide distribution electronic copies	internal messages weighty issues corporate authority record keeping	external messages wide distribution official messages legal documentation
Avoid e-mail for serious or sensitive messages.	*Avoid memos for routine or external messages.*	*Avoid letters for routine business or internal messages.*

Q How should I write?

Follow these best practices whenever you write business correspondence:

- **Address a person** whenever possible, not a title or a department.
- **Be informative** in your subject line or opening sentence.
- **Avoid business jargon.** Be conversational instead.
- **Stress benefits for your reader** whenever possible.
- **Use "you" in positive situations,** but avoid it in negative ones.
- **Use a team approach** (a "we" focus); avoid a "me vs. you" feeling.
- **Use lists, short paragraphs, and white space** to create accessibility.
- **Never send a message written in anger.**

Q What should I include in written correspondence?

In any correspondence that is more complex or formal than a text message or an instant message, you should include an opening, a middle, and a closing. In each part, make sure to answer the receiver's key questions:

FYI In correspondence and comedy, timing is everything. Be certain your message is clear, concise, compelling, and correct—and arrives on time!

Part	Receiver's Question	Your Strategy
Opening	*Why are you writing?*	Give your reason.
Middle	*What should I know?*	Give supporting points.
Closing	*What should I do?*	Outline next steps.

FYI The computer revolution has given businesspeople dozens of new ways to communicate, but all the new gadgetry has also provided dozens of new ways to miscommunicate. No matter which medium you use, the goal should be the same: to send the right message to the right receiver at the right time.

Section 2
Writing Correspondence

In This Section

These chapters provide guidelines and models for each type of business and sales correspondence:

- **Real-Time Correspondence 11**
- **Memos and Faxes 19**
- **Business Letters 25**
- **Sales Correspondence 45**
- **Sales Letters 51**
- **Customer-Service Letters 59**
- **Sales Proposals 67**

2 Creating Real-Time Correspondence

"Time waits for no one." This observation was first made in a medieval play in which Death had come calling for a man's soul. In modern business, the situation is perhaps not as dire—but there are still those "deadlines" and "drop-dead dates" to deal with. No wonder real-time communication is transforming the workplace.

Most business people communicate in a variety of real-time ways: face time, phone time, text messaging, instant messaging, paging, and e-mail.

The intent is always to save time. This chapter will help you make the best use of your real-time correspondence.

Your Goal
Create effective real-time correspondence.

- Understand real-time etiquette.
- Choose the right type of real-time correspondence.
- Create effective e-mail messages.
- Learn to avoid "flame wars."

Q What is real-time correspondence etiquette?

Real-time correspondence etiquette means using your real-time technologies in a polite way for those you are communicating with and for people around you. Follow these tips.

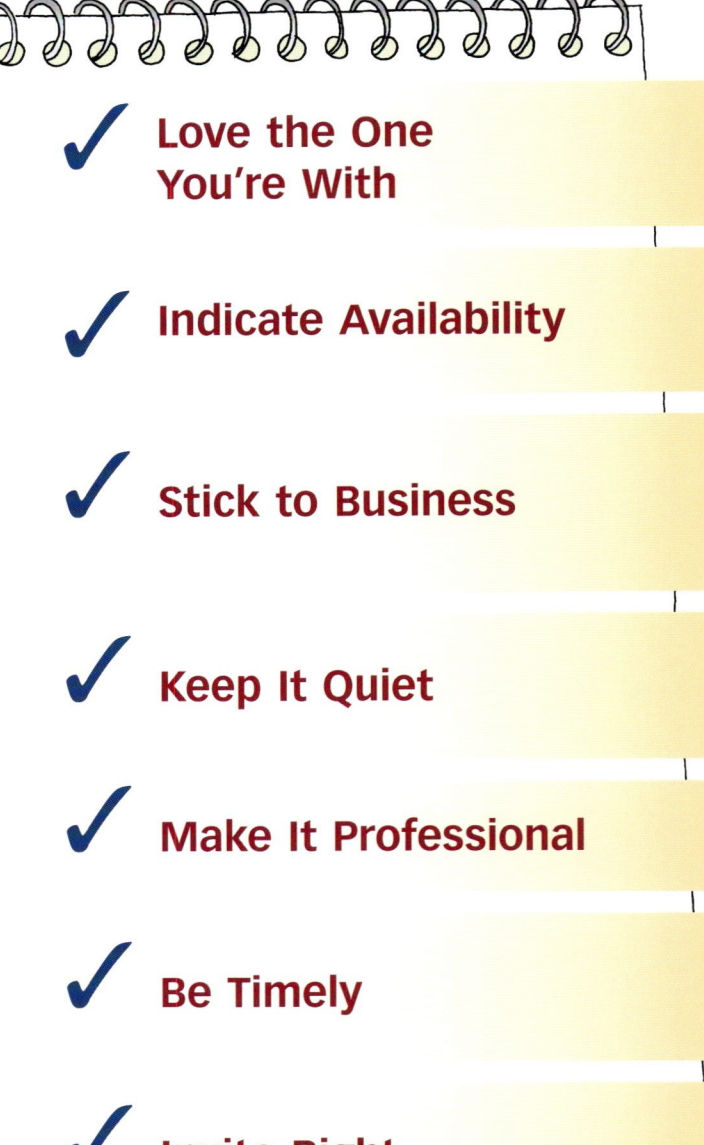

✓ **Love the One You're With**

✓ **Indicate Availability**

✓ **Stick to Business**

✓ **Keep It Quiet**

✓ **Make It Professional**

✓ **Be Timely**

✓ **Invite Right**

- Don't expect a person who is with you to wait while you chat with those who aren't.
- Don't check your wireless e-mail device during a meeting, unless it is important to the meeting.
- Don't let a dinner date sit and chew while you check messages.

- Set your instant messaging (IM) status to inactive when you are away.
- Set your IM status to go inactive after 5 minutes.
- For vacations or long absences, provide automated e-mail responses and voice-mail messages to indicate availability (or lack of it).

- Avoid personal business at work.
- Expect IMs and e-mail to be read by others besides the intended reader. (Such messages may be monitored.)
- Don't IM a colleague while he or she is otherwise busy, such as during an important meeting, or while the person is using a laptop to give a presentation.

- During meetings, presentations, movies, or services, set cell phones and pagers to "silent."
- Make sure incoming message signals and ring tones are not loud or obnoxious.
- If you tend to use a "cell-yell," take the phone call outside.

- Avoid initialisms and emoticons in e-mail, and be careful with them in IM.
- Don't SHOUT (write in all caps).
- Proofread your message before sending it.

- Answer the phone if you can; otherwise, answer the voice mail within an hour.
- Answer instant messages within a few minutes.
- Answer e-mail within a few hours.
- Be patient, giving the other person twice as long to respond as you would take.

- Include only the people who need to receive your message. (Don't copy everyone or IM the whole department.)
- Invite new people to an ongoing conversation only if those involved agree.
- Before forwarding e-mail, make sure it isn't "for your eyes only."

Business and Sales Correspondence

Q: How do businesses use instant messaging?

Businesses use instant messaging (IM) to conduct real-time written conversations. Here are some ways businesses benefit from IM.

Silence	Distance	Delegation	Recording	Monitoring
Teams within open office spaces use IM to share information without disturbing others in the area.	Global teams use IM to conduct real-time discussions inexpensively.	Through IM, a delegate in a meeting can present terms and get responses from an outside decision-maker.	Many IM systems allow conversations to be recorded, and all IM systems allow copying and pasting.	Managers can monitor IM conversations to ensure that workers are on task.

Q: How should I write instant messages?

Successful IMs follow the rules of writing and of conversation.

1. **Politely greet the reader.** Initiate an IM conversation the same way you would initiate a verbal exchange.
2. **Check availability.** Make sure the conversation partner is available before proceeding.
3. **Be concise and clear.** Keep your message brief, but make sure your idea, request, or question is clear.
4. **Be patient.** Different users have different typing speeds, so send your message and wait for a reply. Don't overwhelm your partner with messages.
5. **End well.** When you are finished messaging, provide a clear ending. Also agree with partners that the first person to end an exchange ends it for both.

Note: See the facing page for the anatomy of a successful IM exchange.

Anatomy of a Successful IM

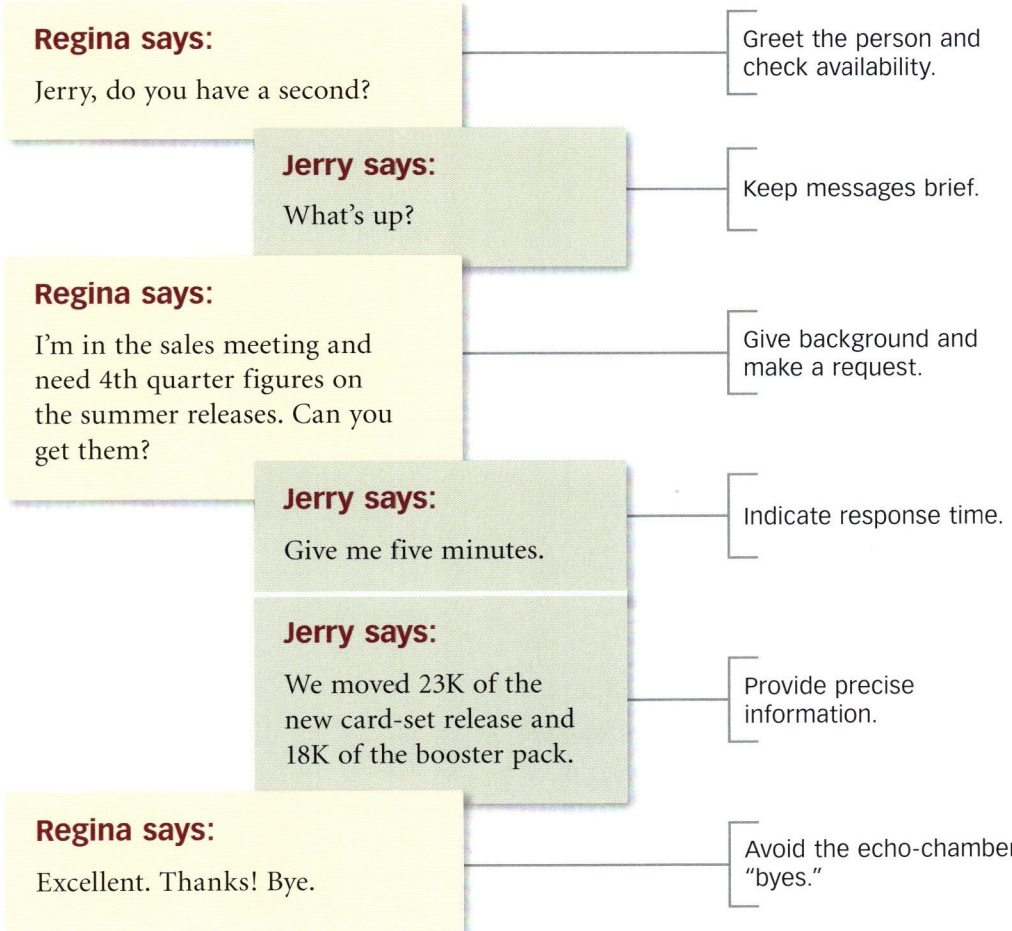

TIP Follow these guidelines whenever you conduct written conversations in real-time, as you would in a Web meeting or a chat room.

Q What guidelines should I follow for e-mail?

Use a stripped-down version of the writing process to quickly create e-mail messages that are clear, concise, compelling, and correct.

1. Prewrite
Analyze the situation.
- *What do I want the receiver to know and do?*
- *How will the receiver feel about the message?*

Gather and organize details.
- *What details should I use, and in what order?*

2. Draft
Provide an informative subject line.
For a complex message, develop three parts:
- **Create an opening.** Greet the receiver and state your reason for writing.
- **Write the middle.** Provide details that the receiver needs.
- **Provide a closing.** Indicate next steps and end politely.

3. Revise
Review your ideas, organization, and voice.
- *Have I included all the necessary information?*
- *Is the information accurate and well organized?*
- *Have I used a friendly but professional voice or tone?*

4. Refine
Check your words, sentences, correctness, and design.
- *Have I selected precise words?*
- *Are my sentences correct?*
- *Have I checked spelling and punctuation?*
- *Have I used short paragraphs and appropriate headings and lists?*

FYI If you are including an attachment, always double-check that it is attached before you hit "send."

BASIC E-MAIL

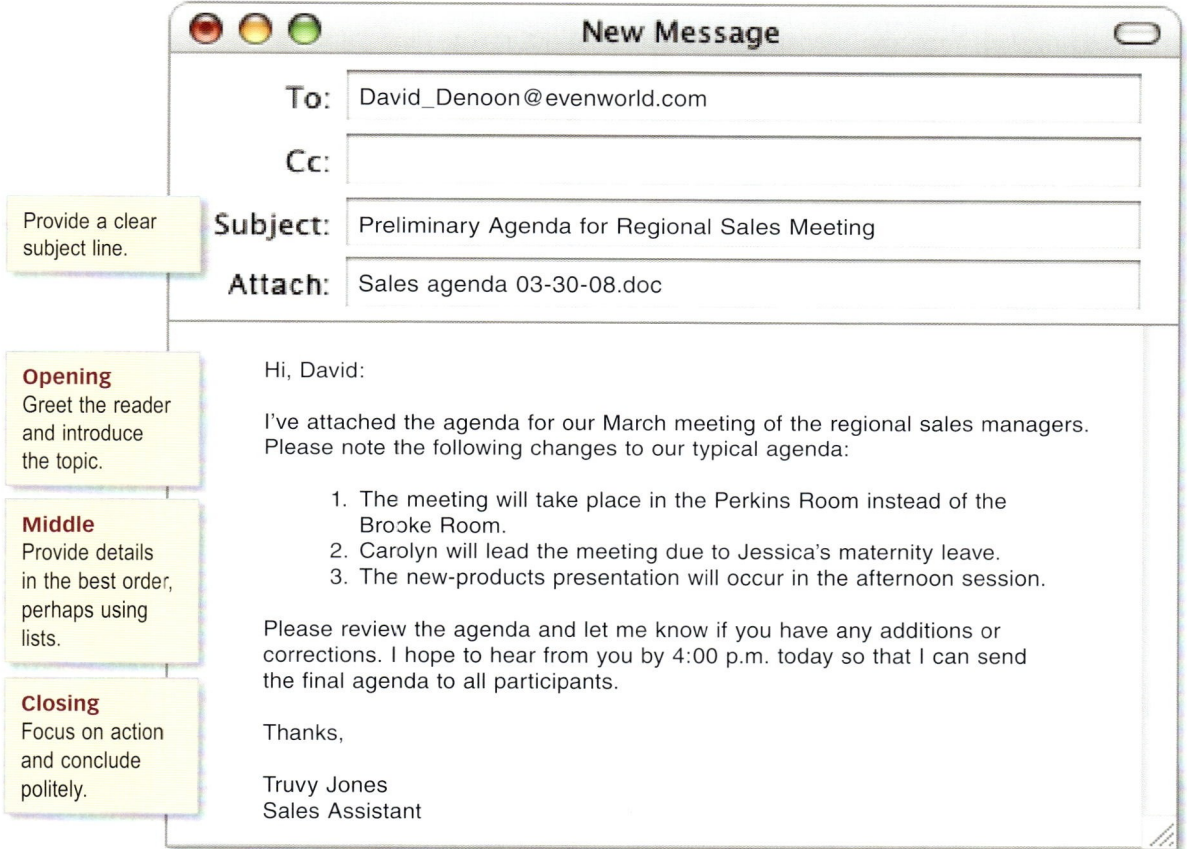

DESIGN TIPS

- Place your greeting on a separate line with a blank line after it.
- Use short paragraphs without indentation.
- Double-space between paragraphs.
- Create numbered or bulleted lists to make information accessible.
- Place a closing on a separate line with your name two lines below.
- If you use a signature line, make sure it reflects well on you and your organization.

Q What are "flame wars"?

"Flame wars" are arguments that develop in written real-time communication and that escalate as time goes on. Often, people caught in flame wars do not understand how the argument began or why it grows worse.

A recent study from the University of Chicago Graduate School of Business found the following causes of most e-mail flame wars:

SENDERS thought their e-mail messages made their feelings clear . . .	**RECEIVERS** thought they understood the senders' feelings . . .	**IN REALITY,** receivers understood senders' feelings only . . .
80 percent of the time.	**90 percent** of the time.	**56 percent** of the time.

One reason flame wars happen is that e-mail does not communicate emotion clearly. Without visual or auditory cues, the receiver is often left to guess the sender's mood and tone of voice—and invent problems.

In personal correspondence, senders sometimes use emoticons [:-), :-(, :-o] to convey their feelings. However, these symbols lack the clarity and formality needed in business e-mail messages.

Q What is the best cure for a flame war?

Prevention is always the best cure for a flame war. Follow these tips to avoid getting into a battle of words.

- Don't use e-mail for emotionally charged issues.
- Never send a message written in anger.
- Be polite in the language you choose (*please, thank you, appreciation, congratulations*). Make positive requests, not negative demands.
- Do not use multiple exclamation points or multiple question marks.
- Do not SHOUT (use all caps).
- Avoid sarcasm, criticism, whining, or laying blame.
- Do not use e-mail to accuse.

If a flame war starts, don't pour more fuel on it by replying with an equally nasty message. Instead, quench the fire by speaking face-to-face or on the phone.

3 Writing Memos and Faxes

Though e-mail has largely replaced memos and faxes, these two types of correspondence still have many valuable uses. For example, memos carry a weight that e-mail does not, and memos prevent sensitive internal information from flying across the world at the click of a mouse. Memos also convey complex information more clearly than e-mail can, with graphics and other formatting strategies that e-mail cannot. For these reasons, writers often compose complex messages as memos and then send them as e-mail attachments.

Faxes remain valuable for sending signed documents, handwritten documents, and any message containing sensitive information, such as financial proposals or legal documents.

Your Goal

Create effective memos and faxes.

- Use the basic memo and fax formats.
- Add formatting elements as needed.
- Provide complete, clear information.

How can I create effective memos?

Follow these steps to develop a memo quickly, clearly, and effectively.

1. **Prewrite**

   Analyze the situation.
   - *What do I want the reader to know and do?*
   - *How will the reader feel about the message?*

   Gather and organize details.
   - *What details does the reader need, and in what order?*

2. **Draft**

   Center "Memo" or "Memorandum" at the top of the page, or provide your company name. Write a subject line that clearly indicates the topic.
   - **Write an opening.** Either state your reason for writing or use a buffer statement (43).
   - **Develop the middle.** Provide details that help the reader understand and respond to your message.
   - **Create a closing.** Clarify any action needed and indicate next steps.

3. **Revise**

   Review the ideas, organization, and voice of your memo.
   - *Have I included all of the important details?*
   - *Have I organized the information logically and clearly?*
   - *Have I used a polite, professional voice?*

4. **Refine**

   Check your words, sentences, correctness, and design.
   - *Have I used precise terminology?*
   - *Do my sentences read smoothly, and are transitions clear?*
   - *Have I used correct punctuation, capitalization, spelling, and grammar? Have I used headings for sections and bulleted or numbered lists to order information?*

> **FYI** Remember that memos are for internal correspondence. To send a message to someone outside your organization, use e-mail or a business letter.

BASIC MEMO

Center "Memo" or company name.
Complete heading lines and add initials.
Create a subject line.

Memo

Date: April 26, 2008

To: Tammy Augustyn

From: Rob King RK *Double- or single-space heading.*

Subject: Braille edition of *The Newcastle Handbook*

Triple Space

Opening
Provide your reason for writing.

Slenkman Publishing has received a request to create a Braille edition of *The Newcastle Handbook*. Please burn the following files to disks that we can send to the specialty printer:

- InDesign files of *The Newcastle Handbook*
- PDF files of the handbook
- A list of file names for each version of the book

Double Space

Middle
Give details that answer the reader's main questions.

Also, please prepare a UPS 2nd day air package to send both disks and the lists to the following person:

Andrea Reynolds
Composition Buyer
Slenkman Publishing
583 Beacon Street
Boston, MA 02116
(617) 355-5555

Closing
Focus on next steps and thank the reader.

Please charge this UPS package to the Slenkman Publishing account.

Would it be possible to complete these tasks by 1:30 tomorrow (Friday) in time for the UPS pickup? Thanks for your help!

Use 1" to 1.5" margins and block style.

Q How should I format an expanded memo?

When a memo requires more than one page or includes additional elements, follow the instructions below and the model on the facing page.

HEADING

1 You can type the word *Memo, Memorandum,* or the company name at the top, but do not include the company's address or phone number.

2 For sensitive messages, label your memo *CONFIDENTIAL* and seal it in an envelope that is also marked *CONFIDENTIAL.*

3 Complete your heading with job titles, phone numbers, e-mail addresses, or a checklist showing the memo's purpose. Initial the memo after your name in the heading. If you have more than one reader, use one of these options:

- List the names after *To:* and highlight a different one on each copy of the memo.
- Type *See distribution* after *To:* and list all the readers at the end of the memo.
- Type a department's name after *To:*

CLOSING

4 Use quick-response options such as checklists, fill-in-the-blanks, or boxes.

5 Add an identification line showing the initials of who wrote the memo (in caps) and who typed it (in lowercase), separated by a slash.

6 If you're sending documents with the memo, type *Attachment(s)* or *Enclosure(s),* followed by either (a) the number of documents or (b) a colon and the document titles listed vertically.

7 If you want to send copies to secondary readers, type *c* or *cc* and a colon; then list the names and job titles stacked vertically (when job titles are included). To send a copy to someone without the main reader knowing it, add *bc* (blind copy) ONLY on the copy sent to the person listed after this notation.

Darcy Mohr   Page 2   July 3, 2008

Page 2
Darcy Mohr
July 3, 2008

FYI If your memo is longer than one page, carry over at least two lines of the message onto a plain sheet of stationery. Use one of the heading formats shown on the left.

EXPANDED MEMO

[1] Triplett International, LLP

[2] CONFIDENTIAL

Date: July 3, 2008

[3] To: Tracy Schenk, Vice President of Human Resources
              See distribution.

DM

From: Darcy Mohr, Manager of Shipping and Receiving

Subject: Richard Dutton

Several weeks ago, I suspected that Richard Dutton, one of our drivers, had been drinking on the job. Today, I learned that he has received three citations for "driving under the influence" (DUI) over the last four years—most recently last Friday. I have attached proof of this, which I found on the Internet.

As Triplett's *Employee Handbook* states, "A driver who receives a DUI must report the incident to HR within four days after the incident." Richard's file includes no record of any DUI.

I propose the following:

1. Nancy Chen and I will speak with Richard about his DUI's and Triplett's related policy.

2. Following the meeting, Nancy and I will meet with you to report on our conversation with Richard and to propose follow-up action.

[4] Please initial below and return the memo by interoffice courier.

I have read this memo and will reply as soon as possible _____.
                                                    Initial here.

[5] DM/gh
[6] Attachment: MADD police blotter
[7] cc: Mark Moon, Warehouse Manager
       Nancy Chen, Union Representative

24 Business and Sales Correspondence

Q How should I format a fax cover sheet?

Use your organization's cover sheet or a format from your word-processing program, or create your own cover sheet with some or all of the items below.

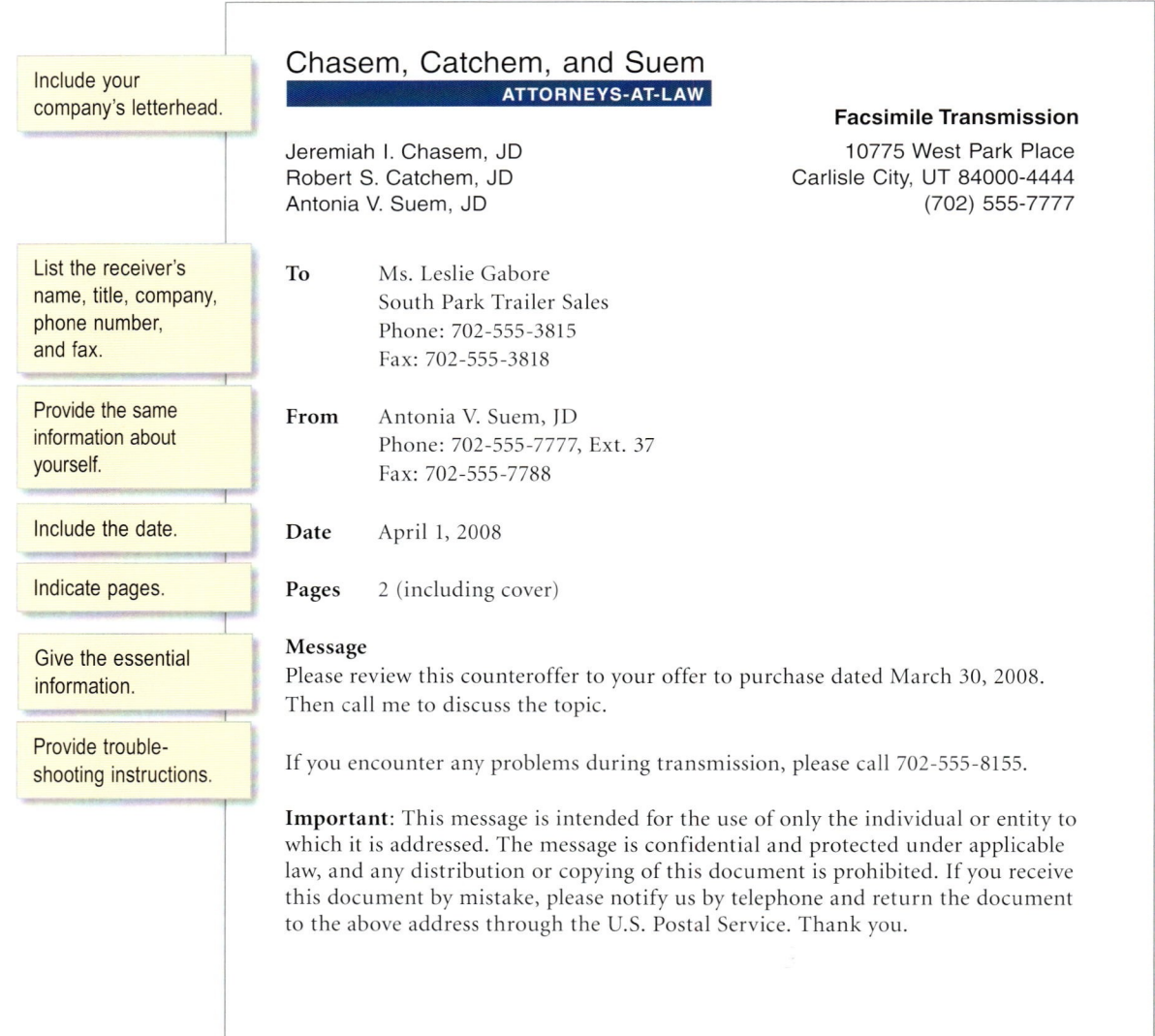

- Include your company's letterhead.
- List the receiver's name, title, company, phone number, and fax.
- Provide the same information about yourself.
- Include the date.
- Indicate pages.
- Give the essential information.
- Provide troubleshooting instructions.

Chasem, Catchem, and Suem
ATTORNEYS-AT-LAW

Jeremiah I. Chasem, JD
Robert S. Catchem, JD
Antonia V. Suem, JD

Facsimile Transmission
10775 West Park Place
Carlisle City, UT 84000-4444
(702) 555-7777

To Ms. Leslie Gabore
South Park Trailer Sales
Phone: 702-555-3815
Fax: 702-555-3818

From Antonia V. Suem, JD
Phone: 702-555-7777, Ext. 37
Fax: 702-555-7788

Date April 1, 2008

Pages 2 (including cover)

Message
Please review this counteroffer to your offer to purchase dated March 30, 2008. Then call me to discuss the topic.

If you encounter any problems during transmission, please call 702-555-8155.

Important: This message is intended for the use of only the individual or entity to which it is addressed. The message is confidential and protected under applicable law, and any distribution or copying of this document is prohibited. If you receive this document by mistake, please notify us by telephone and return the document to the above address through the U.S. Postal Service. Thank you.

4 Writing Business Letters

Thousands of years ago, business letters were written in cuneiform on clay tablets, which were then fired in a kiln before being sent. These business letters allowed merchants to trade goods with others hundreds or thousands of miles away.

Today, electronic communication handles most written correspondence. However, the business letter remains the best form for certain messages, particularly those that are long or serious or that contain bad news. This chapter will help you determine when and how to write effective letters.

Your Goal

Create letters that take care of serious business.

- Use the writing process to perfect your message.
- Follow correct format for letters and envelopes.
- Employ appropriate forms of address.

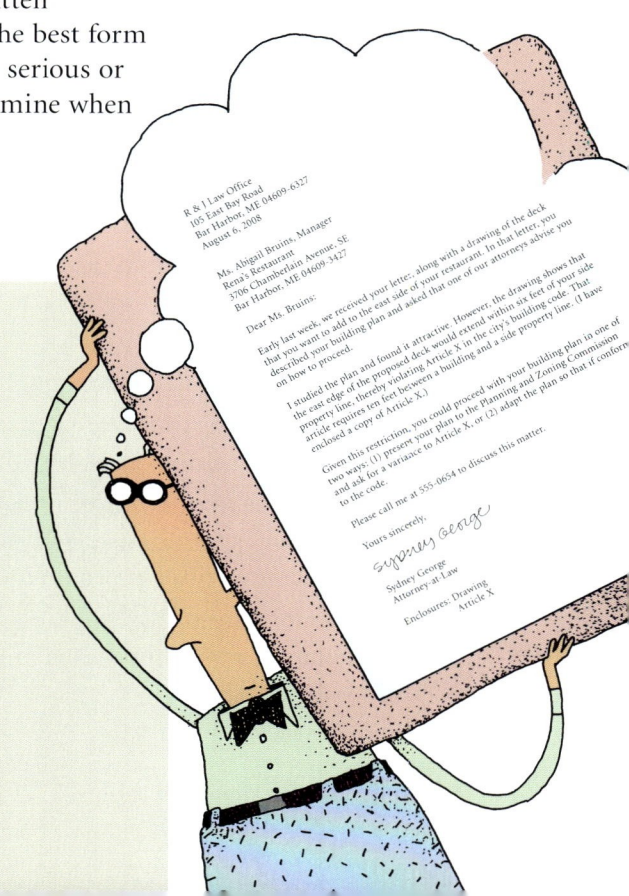

Q When should I write a letter?

Write a letter for official company correspondence with those outside of your organization. (Use a memo for those within the company.) Though e-mail can also be used for outside correspondence, a letter may serve better in the situations described below.

Write a formal business letter for . . .

1. **Long messages.** E-mail is meant to be short. If the message is long and complicated, a letter will convey your point more clearly.
2. **Official communications.** When speaking for your organization or relaying weighty news, use a letter to make the message clear and formal.
3. **Legal notices.** For legal matters, write a letter.
4. **Persuasive appeals.** To convince someone to make an important business decision, write a letter—and follow it up with a phone call or an e-mail.
5. **Sales letters.** With customers sick of spam, use sales letters (**45–58**) to communicate your personal and professional concerns.
6. **Bad-news messages.** When you must break serious bad news, a formal letter is more appropriate than an e-mail message.
7. **Letters of appreciation.** When you want to thank a business partner, a formal letter means much more than an e-mail.
8. **Confidential information.** To provide information for the reader's eyes only, the business letter is still the correspondence of choice.
9. **Résumés and applications.** Though many organizations request online applications, always follow up your electronic correspondence with a prompt and polished letter.
10. **Commemorations.** To send a message that may be kept in commemoration—such as a certificate of achievement or a diploma—use a business letter.

How can the writing process improve my letters?

The writing process helps you create clear, concise, and compelling letters. Follow these guidelines:

1. **Prewrite**

    Analyze the situation.
    - *What do I want the letter to accomplish?*
    - *What are the reader's concerns, and what does the reader know?*
    - *How is the reader connected to my organization?*

    Gather and organize details.
    - *What is my main point?*
    - *What supporting points should I make, and in what order?*
    - *What documents or files contain needed details?*

2. **Draft**

    Use a correct letter format. (See page 33.)
    - **Write an opening.** State the situation (for good or neutral news), begin with a buffer (for bad news), or capture your reader's interest (for persuasive messages).
    - **Develop the middle** with supporting points and explanations.
    - **Create a closing** with a call to action (who should do what, when).

3. **Revise**

    Review your letter's ideas, organization, and voice.
    - *Are all names, dates, and details correct and accurate?*
    - *Does information appear in a logical order?*
    - *Do I use a conversational but professional tone?*
    - *Have I used personal pronouns in a positive way (or not at all)?*

4. **Refine**

    Check your words, sentences, correctness, and design.
    - *Do my sentences pass the "read aloud" test?*
    - *Have I used correct punctuation, capitalization, spelling, and grammar?*
    - *Have I followed a consistent and correct letter format?*

Q How should I format a basic business letter?

Follow these guidelines:

- Do not indent paragraphs.
- Single-space within paragraphs.
- Double-space between paragraphs.
- Leave the right margin ragged (uneven).
- Set margins from 1 to 1.5 inches.

1 The **heading** provides the reader a return address. Type the address (minus the writer's name) at the top of the letter. Spell out words like *Road, Street, West. Note:* Omit the address if you are using a letterhead.

2 The **date** shows when the letter was drafted or dictated. Write the date as month, day, year for U.S. correspondence (August 6, 2008); write day, month, year for international or military correspondence (6 August 2008).

3 The **inside address** gives the reader's name and complete mailing address. Type it flush left and include as many details as necessary, in this order:

- reader's courtesy title, name, and job title (if the job title is one word)
- reader's job title (if two or more words)
- office or department
- organization name
- street address/p.o. box/suite/room
- city, state, zip code (or city, country, postal code)

4 The **salutation** personalizes the message. Capitalize all first letters and place a colon after the name. (See pages 34–37.)

5 The **body** contains the message, usually organized into three parts:

- an opening that states why you are writing,
- a middle that gives details the reader needs, and
- a closing that focuses on what should happen next.

6 The **complimentary closing** provides a polite word or phrase to end the message. Capitalize the first word only and add a comma after the closing.

7 The **signature block** makes the letter official. Align the writer's name with the complimentary closing. Place a one-word job title on the same line as the typed name or below the name; place a longer title below the typed name.

8 Use an **enclosure note** whenever you enclose something. Type *Enclosure(s)* or *Enc(s).* and the number of enclosures. To list enclosures by name, type *Enclosure(s)* or *Enc(s).*, a colon, and the names stacked vertically:

Enclosures: Article
              Drawing

BASIC LETTER

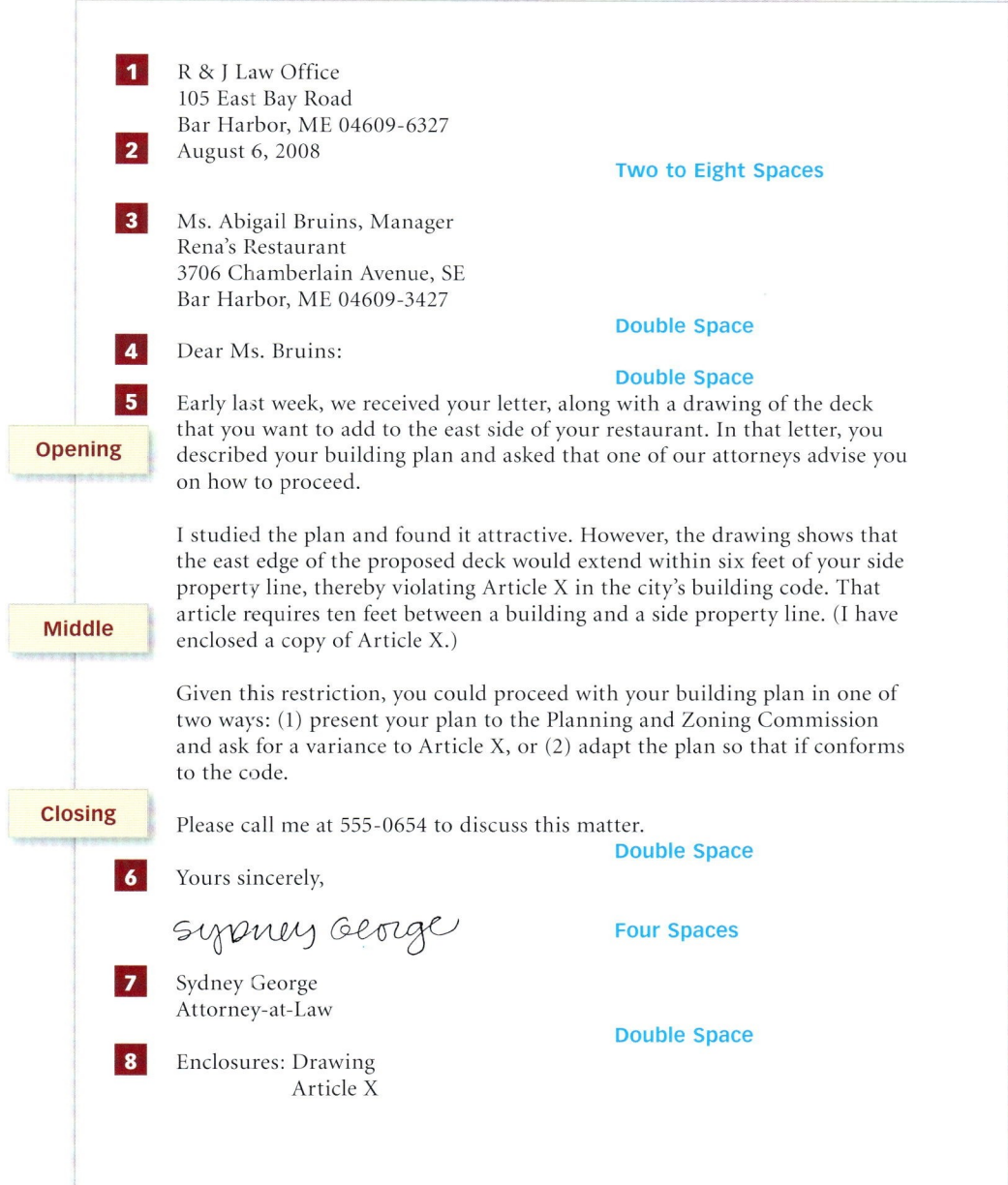

Q How should I format an expanded business letter?

When you, your reader, a typist, a filing clerk, or future readers need additional information, include one or more of the items from this list:

1 A **method of transmission note** indicates how a letter should be or has been sent: *via facsimile, via registered mail, via overnight courier.*

2 A **reference line** begins with a guide word and a colon (*Reference:* or *In reply to:*) followed by a file, an account, an invoice, or a database number.

3 When appropriate, use a **confidential notation** on both the letter and the envelope. CAPITALIZE or underline the word *confidential* for emphasis.

4 In the **inside address**, stack names by alphabet or position for two or more readers. For two readers at separate addresses, stack the addresses (including names) with a line between.

5 The **attention line** designates a reader or department but encourages others to read the letter. Place it two lines below the inside address, flush left or centered. CAPITALIZE or underline for emphasis.

6 The **subject line** announces the topic and is placed flush left two lines below the attention line. CAPITALIZE or underline for emphasis.

7 The **signature block** may include the writer's courtesy title typed in front of the name to clarify his or her gender or a preferred form of address.

8 In the **identification line**, type the writer's initials in capitals and the typist's in lowercase, separated by a slash (but no spaces).

9 Use the **copies notation** by typing *c* or *cc*, followed by a colon and a vertical list of people (with job titles in parentheses). To send a copy to someone else without the reader knowing it, type *bc* or *bcc* (blind copy), but only on the copy sent to the person listed.

10 **Continuation pages** follow a letter's first page. On blank stationery, carry over at least two lines and use a heading in one of the formats below:

Page 2
Gloria P. Walsch
Paul DiDomenico
September 4, 2008   **10**

Gloria P. Walsch   Page 2   September 4, 2008
Paul DiDomenico

EXPANDED LETTER

 **R&J Law Office**
105 East Bay Road, Bar Harbor, ME 04609-6327 • 207-555-0645 • rjlawoffice.com

August 6, 2008

Two to Eight Spaces

1 Via facsimile

Double Space

2 Reference: A. Bruins #2

Double Space

3 CONFIDENTIAL

Double Space

4 Ms. Abigail Bruins
Mr. Paul Meyer
Rena's Restaurant
3706 Chamberlain Avenue, SE
Bar Harbor, ME 04609-3427

Double Space

5 <u>Attention:</u> Ms. Bruins and Mr. Meyer

Double Space

6 BUILDING PERMIT

Double Space

Early last week, we received your letter, along with a drawing of the deck that you want to add to the east side of your restaurant. I studied the plan and found it attractive. However, the drawing shows that the proposed deck would extend within six feet of your side-property line, thereby violating Article X in the city's building code. That article requires ten feet between a building and a side-property line.

Given this restriction, you could proceed with your building plan in one of two ways: (1) present your plan to the Planning and Zoning Commission and ask for a variance to Article X, or (2) adapt the plan so that it conforms to the code. Please call me at 555-0654 to discuss this matter.

Yours sincerely,

Double Space

Sydney George

Four Spaces

7 Ms. Sydney George
Attorney-at-Law

Double Space

8 SG/mbb
Enclosures 2
9 cc: Leah Theodore (Senior Partner)

What letter formats can I choose from?

You can use full-block, semiblock, or simplified format.

Full-Block Format

Rules:	All parts flush left
Character:	Professional, clean, contemporary
Plus:	Easy to set up and follow
Minus:	May appear unbalanced to the left of the page
Best Uses:	Routine letters
Note:	A more traditional or international reader may not like this format.

Semiblock Format

Rules:	Date line, method of transmission line, reference line, complimentary closing, and signature block align with a vertical line at the center of the page; all other parts flush left
Character:	Professional, traditional
Plus:	Balanced appearance on the page
Minus:	More difficult setup than full-block or simplified
Best Uses:	International, traditional, and social letters
Note:	You may indent the subject line and all paragraphs to further soften the form. In addition, you may drop the space between paragraphs.

Simplified Format

Rules:	All parts flush left No salutation or complimentary closing Subject line and writer's name in caps; dash between the writer's name and title
Character:	Bare-bones, functional
Plus:	Easy setup
Minus:	Impersonal format due to lack of courtesy elements
Best Uses:	Routine letters—regular reminders, notices, bulletins, orders, mass mailings Not appropriate for high-level or persuasive letters
Note:	You may drop courtesy titles from the inside address.

Writing Business Letters

FULL BLOCK

R & J Law Office
105 East Bay Road, Bar Harbor, ME 04609-6327
207-555-0654   rjlawoffice.com

August 6, 2008

Reference: A. Bruins #2

CONFIDENTIAL

Ms. Abigail Bruins
Mr. Paul Meyer
Rena's Restaurant
3706 Chamberlain Avenue, SE
Bar Harbor, ME 04609-3427

Dear Ms. Bruins and Mr. Meyer:

BUILDING PERMIT

Early last week, we received your letter, along with drawings of the deck that you want to add to the east side of your restaurant. In that letter, you described your building plan and asked that one of our attorneys advise you on how to proceed.

I studied the plan and found it attractive. However, the drawings show that the east edge of the proposed deck would extend within six feet of your side-property line, thereby violating Article X in the city's building code. That article requires ten feet between a building and a side-property line.

Given this restriction, you could proceed with your building plan in one of two ways: (1) present your plan to the Planning and Zoning Commission and ask for a variance to Article X, or (2) adapt the plan so that it conforms to the code.

Please call me at 555-0654 to discuss this matter.

Yours sincerely,

Sydney George

Ms. Sydney George
Attorney-at-Law

SG/mbb
Enc.: Drawing
       Article X
cc: Leah Theodore (Senior Partner)

SEMIBLOCK

R & J Law Office
105 East Bay Road, Bar Harbor, ME 04609-6327
207-555-0654   rjlawoffice.com

August 6, 2008

Reference: A. Bruins #2

CONFIDENTIAL

Ms. Abigail Bruins
Mr. Paul Meyer
Rena's Restaurant
3706 Chamberlain Avenue, SE
Bar Harbor, ME 04609-3427

Dear Ms. Bruins and Mr. Meyer:

BUILDING PERMIT

Early last week, we received your letter, along with drawings of the deck that you want to add to the east side of your restaurant. In that letter, you described your building plan and asked that one of our attorneys advise you on how to proceed.

I studied the plan and found it attractive. However, the drawings show that the east edge of the proposed deck would extend within six feet of your side-property line, thereby violating Article X in the city's building code. That article requires ten feet between a building and a side-property line.

Given this restriction, you could proceed with your building plan in one of two ways: (1) present your plan to the Planning and Zoning Commission and ask for a variance to Article X, or (2) adapt the plan so that it conforms to the code.

Please call me at 555-0654 to discuss this matter.

Yours sincerely,

Sydney George

Ms. Sydney George
Attorney-at-Law

SG/mbb
Enc.: Drawing
       Article X
cc: Leah Theodore (Senior Partner)

SIMPLIFIED

R & J Law Office
105 East Bay Road, Bar Harbor, ME 04609-6327
207-555-0665   rjlawoffice.com

August 6, 2008

Reference: A. Bruins #2

CONFIDENTIAL

Abigail Bruins
Paul Meyer
Rena's Restaurant
3706 Chamberlain Avenue, SE
Bar Harbor, ME 04609-3427

BUILDING PERMIT

Early last week, we received your letter, along with drawings of the deck that you want to add to the east side of your restaurant. In that letter, you described your building plan and asked that one of our attorneys advise you on how to proceed.

I studied the plan and found it attractive. However, the drawings show that the east edge of the proposed deck would extend within six feet of your side-property line, thereby violating Article X in the city's building code. That article requires ten feet between a building and a side-property line.

Given this restriction, you could proceed with your building plan in one of two ways: (1) present your plan to the Planning and Zoning Commission and ask for a variance to Article X, or (2) adapt the plan so that it conforms to the code.

Please call me at 555-0654 to discuss this matter.

Sydney George

MS. SYDNEY GEORGE—ATTORNEY-AT-LAW

SG/mbb
Enc.: Drawing
       Article X
cc: Leah Theodore (Senior Partner)

How can I address my reader with respect?

Use the guidelines below and on the following pages to find a fitting title and salutation.

PROFESSIONAL TITLES

	Titles in Address	
Business		
CEO	Ms. Sarah Falwell Chief Executive Officer	Dear Ms. Falwell:
Vice President	Dr. David Levengood Vice President	Dear Dr. Levengood:
Company Official	Ms. Susan Cook, Comptroller	Dear Ms. Cook:
Education		
President or Chancellor of University (Ph.D.)	Dr. Joe Smith, President	Dear Dr. Smith: (or) Dear President Smith:
Dean of a School or College (Ph.D.)	Dr. Marjorie Stone, Dean School of Life Sciences	Dear Dr. Stone: (or) Dear Dean Stone:
Professor (Ph.D.)	Dr. Patricia Monk Professor of Psychology	Dear Dr. Monk: (or) Dear Professor Monk:
Instructor (no Ph.D.)	Mr. Art Linkman Instructor of Physics	Dear Mr. Linkman:
Legal		
Lawyer	Mr. Daniel Walker Attorney-at-Law (or) Daniel Walker, Esq.	Dear Mr. Walker: (or) Dear Daniel Walker, Esq.:
Medical		
Physician	Dr. Sarah McDonald (or) Sarah McDonald, M.D.	Dear Dr. McDonald:
Registered Nurse	Nurse John Seguin (or) John Seguin, R.N.	Dear Nurse Seguin:
Dentist	Dr. Leslie Matheson (or) Leslie Matheson, D.D.S.	Dear Dr. Matheson:
Veterinarian	Dr. Manuel Ortega (or) Manuel Ortega, D.V.M.	Dear Dr. Ortega:

Professional Titles

- Avoid writing to positions, titles, or departments. Call the organization (or visit its Web site) for names.
- Spell out all professional titles except **Dr.** and **Esq.**
- Avoid using two professional titles that mean the same thing: *Dr. Paula Felch, M.D.*

MALE, FEMALE, MULTIPLE, AND UNNAMED READERS

	Titles in Address	Salutations
One Woman (avoid showing marital status)		
Preferred	Ms. Barbara Jordan	Dear Ms. Jordan:
Married or Widowed	Mrs. Lorene Frost	Dear Mrs. Frost:
Single	Miss Adriana Langille	Dear Miss Langille:
Two or More Women (alphabetical)		
Standard	Ms. Bethany Jergens Ms. Shavonn Mitchell	Dear Ms. Jergens and Ms. Mitchell:
Formal	Mmes. Bethany Jergens and Shavonn Mitchell	Dear Mmes. Jergens and Mitchell:
One Man		
Standard	Mr. Hugh Knight	Dear Mr. Knight:
With Jr., Sr., or Roman Numeral	Mr. Brian Boswell Jr. (or) Mr. Brian Boswell III	Dear Mr. Boswell:
Two or More Men (alphabetical)		
Standard	Mr. Alex Fernandez Mr. Nate Shaw	Dear Mr. Fernandez and Mr. Shaw:
Formal	Messrs. Alex Fernandez and Nate Shaw	Dear Messrs. Fernandez and Shaw:
One Man and One Woman (alphabetical)		
	Ms. Paula Trunhope Mr. Joe Williams	Dear Ms. Trunhope and Mr. Williams:
Married Couple		
Same Last Name	Mr. William and Mrs. Susan Lui	Dear Mr. and Mrs. Lui:
Different Last Names	Mr. William Bentley Ms. Sinead Sweeney	Dear Mr. Bentley and Ms. Sweeney:
One Reader (gender unknown)		
	M. Robin Leeds (or) Robin Leeds	Dear M. Leeds: (or) Dear Robin Leeds:
Mixed Group		
Company, Department, Job Title, or Unknown Reader	Acme Corporation Human Resources Dept.	Formal **Dear Sir or Madam:** Informal **Dear Manager:**

Courtesy Titles

- Choose "standard" or "formal" titles and salutations based on your relationship with the reader and the seriousness of the message.

- Abbreviate all courtesy titles: **Mr., Ms., Mrs.**

- Never guess your reader's gender (*Robin, Pat, Chris*).

GOVERNMENT OFFICIALS AND REPRESENTATIVES

To address government officials, follow this pattern:

Title in Inside Address:	The Honorable *(full name)* *(full title on second line)*
Formal Salutation:	Dear Sir/Madam: or Dear Mr./Madam *(position)*:
Informal Salutation:	Dear Mr./Ms. *(last name)*: or Dear *(position) (last name)*:

	Titles in Address	Salutations
National		
President	The President	Dear Mr./Madam President:
Vice President	The Vice President	Dear Mr. Vice President:
Speaker of the House	The Honorable Steven Kudo	Dear Mr. Speaker:
Cabinet Members, Undersecretaries, etc.	The Honorable Jane Dees	Dear Madam: (or) Dear Attorney General Dees:
Senators (U.S. or State)	The Honorable Bill Johnson	Dear Senator Johnson:
Representatives (U.S. or State)	The Honorable Joan Walker	Dear Ms. Walker: (or) Dear Representative Walker:
Heads of Offices and Agencies	The Honorable John Hillman Postmaster General	Dear Mr. Postmaster General: (or) Dear Mr. Hillman:
Chief Justice (U.S. or State)	The Honorable Shelby Woo Chief Justice of California	Dear Madam Chief Justice:
U.S. Ambassador	The Honorable Francis del Verda	Dear Madam Ambassador: (or) Dear Ambassador del Verda:
State/Local		
Governor	The Honorable Mary Lee	Dear Governor Lee:
Mayor	The Honorable Mark Barne	Dear Mayor Barne:
Council Member	The Honorable Corey Springs	Dear Mr. Springs:
Judge	The Honorable Grace Kim	Dear Judge Kim:
Military		
General	Major General Karl P. Bastion, USAF	Formal **Sir**: Informal **Dear General Bastion**:
Lieutenant	Lieutenant Jane Evans, USMC	Dear Ms. Evans:

Official Titles

- Use a formal title (**Senator, General**) rather than a standard courtesy title (*Mr., Ms.*).
- Avoid outdated courtesy forms (*Gentlemen, To Whom It May Concern*).

RELIGIOUS TITLES

To address religious leaders from any faith with titles that fit their positions, follow these guidelines.

	Titles in Address	Salutations
Roman Catholic Clergy		
Cardinal	His Eminence, Edward Cardinal Romero	Your Eminence: (or) Dear Cardinal Romero:
Archbishop and Bishop	The Most Reverend Henri Crétien	Your Excellency: (or) Dear Bishop/Archbishop Crétien:
Priest	The Reverend Morris Franklin	Reverend Sir: (or) Dear Father Franklin:
Nun	Sister Mary Jennsen	Dear Sister Mary: (or) Dear Sister Jennsen:
Monk	Brother Atticus Bartholemew	Dear Brother Atticus: (or) Dear Brother Bartholemew:
Protestant Clergy		
Bishop (Anglican, Episcopal, Methodist)	The Right Reverend Samuel Wolfe	Right Reverend Sir: (or) Reverend Sir: (or) Dear Bishop Wolfe:
Dean (Head of Cathedral or Seminary)	The Very Reverend Nicholas Cameron	Very Reverend Sir: (or) Dear Dean Cameron:
Minister or Priest	The Reverend Susan Edwards (or) Pastor Edwards	Dear Reverend Edwards: (or) Dear Pastor Edwards:
Chaplain	Chaplain Adam Carp Captain, USMC	Dear Chaplain Carp:
Jewish Clergy		
Rabbi	Rabbi Joshua Gould	Dear Rabbi Gould:
Rabbi with Doctor of Divinity Degree	Rabbi Joshua Gould, D.D.	Dear Dr. Gould:

Religious Titles

- The use of *The* before *Reverend* differs from church to church. Follow the organization's preference.

- In some religious orders, the title in the salutation is followed by the reader's first name. Other orders prefer the last name.

- If the person has a doctor of divinity degree, add a comma and *D.D.* after his or her name in the address (not in the salutation).

Q How should I fold letters?

Create a fold that matches the paper and envelope:

A Standard Envelope: To put a letter in its matching envelope, place the letter faceup and follow these steps:

1. Fold the bottom edge up so that the paper is divided into thirds. Use your thumbnail to create a clean crease.
2. Fold the top third down over the bottom third, leaving 1/4 inch for easy unfolding, and crease firmly.
3. Insert the letter (with the open end at the top) into the envelope.

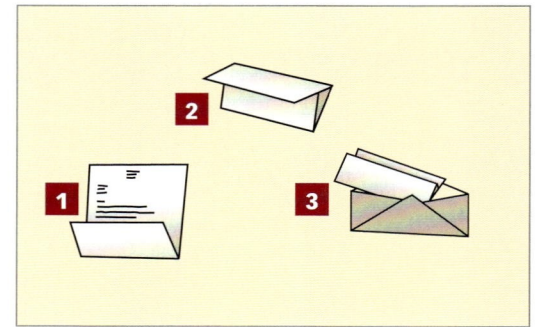

A Small Envelope: If you must place a letter in a small envelope, follow these steps:

1. Fold the bottom edge up so that the paper is divided in half, and create a clean crease.
2. Fold the right side to the left so that the sheet is divided into thirds; crease firmly.
3. Fold the left third over the right third and crease firmly.
4. Turn the letter sideways and insert it (with the open end at the top) into the envelope.

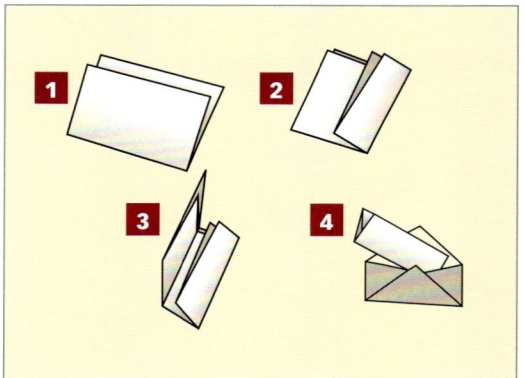

A Window Envelope: Position the inside address on the letter so that it will show through the window. Then place the letter faceup and fold it as follows:

1. Fold the bottom edge up so that the paper is divided into thirds, and create a clean crease.
2. Turn the letter facedown with the top edge toward you and fold the top third of the letter back.
3. Insert the letter in the envelope and make sure that the whole address shows through the window.

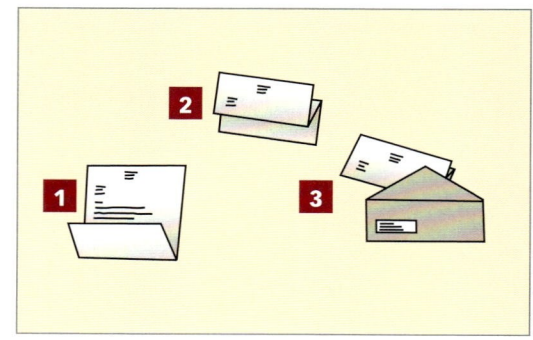

Q How should I address envelopes?

To be sure that your letters are delivered quickly and correctly, follow all United States Postal Service (USPS) guidelines when you address an envelope.

1. Type the sender's name and address using an all-cap style. Make sure all lines are horizontal and lined up flush left. Leave out all punctuation except the hyphen in the zip code.
2. Type the receiver's address—including the type of street (ST, AVE), compass points (NE, SW), and full zip code—in the order pictured. Place the suite, room, or apartment number on the address line, after the street address.
3. Use USPS abbreviations for states and other words in the address. Use numerals rather than words for numbered streets (9TH AVE). Add zip+4 codes. (Go to www.usps.com to get the zip code for any street address in the United States.)

TIPS FOR INTERNATIONAL MAIL

When sending international mail, print the country name alone on the last line. As long as the country, city, and state or province are in English, the name and address may be in the language of the country listed.

Pattern: Name of Receiver
Street Address or PO Box
City, State/Province, Code
Country (Caps, English)

Examples:

MR BRUCE WARNER
2431 EDEN WAY
LONDON W1P 4HQ
ENGLAND

MS TAMARA BEALS
56 METCALFE CRES
MONTREAL QC J7V 8P2
CANADA

What standard abbreviations should I use?

STATES, PROVINCES, AND TERRITORIES

U.S. States							
Alabama	AL	Kansas	KS	Ohio	OH	**Canadian Provinces, Territories**	
Alaska	AK	Kentucky	KY	Oklahoma	OK		
Arizona	AZ	Louisiana	LA	Oregon	OR		
Arkansas	AR	Maine	ME	Pennsylvania	PA	Alberta	AB
California	CA	Maryland	MD	Puerto Rico	PR	British Columbia	BC
Colorado	CO	Massachusetts	MA	Rhode Island	RI	Manitoba	MB
Connecticut	CT	Michigan	MI	South Carolina	SC	New Brunswick	NB
Delaware	DE	Minnesota	MN	South Dakota	SD	Newfoundland and Labrador	NL
District of Columbia	DC	Mississippi	MS	Tennessee	TN		
		Missouri	MO	Texas	TX	Northwest Territories	NT
Florida	FL	Montana	MT	Utah	UT		
Georgia	GA	Nebraska	NE	Vermont	VT	Nova Scotia	NS
Guam	GU	Nevada	NV	Virginia	VA	Nunavut	NU
Hawaii	HI	New Hampshire	NH	Virgin Islands	VI	Ontario	ON
Idaho	ID	New Jersey	NJ	Washington	WA	Prince Edward Island	PE
Illinois	IL	New Mexico	NM	West Virginia	WV		
Indiana	IN	New York	NY	Wisconsin	WI	Quebec	QC
Iowa	IA	North Carolina	NC	Wyoming	WY	Saskatchewan	SK
		North Dakota	ND			Yukon Territory	YT

ABBREVIATIONS FOR USE ON ENVELOPES

Annex	ANX	Lake	LK	Route	RTE
Apartment	APT	Lakes	LKS	Rural	R
Avenue	AVE	Lane	LN	Rural Route	RR
Boulevard	BLVD	Meadows	MDWS	Shore	SH
Building	BLDG	North	N	South	S
Causeway	CSWY	Northeast	NE	Southeast	SE
Circle	CIR	Northwest	NW	Southwest	SW
Court	CT	Office	OFC	Square	SQ
Drive	DR	Palms	PLMS	Station	STA
East	E	Park	PARK	Street	ST
Expressway	EXPY	Parkway	PKWY	Suite	STE
Floor	FL	Place	PL	Terrace	TER
Fort	FT	Plaza	PLZ	Throughway	TRWY
Freeway	FWY	Port	PRT	Turnpike	TPKE
Harbor	HBR	Post Office Box	PO BOX	Union	UN
Heights	HTS	Ridge	RDG	Viaduct	VIA
Highway	HWY	River	RIV	View	VW
Hospital	HOSP	Road	RD	Village	VLG
Junction	JCT	Room	RM	West	W

FYI For mass mailings, check the Postal Service's bar-coding and mailing-list services for speed and savings. Go to www.usps.com.

5 Organizing with Purpose

What do you do when you have *good news* to share? You simply blurt it out: "Hey, everybody, we got the Jenkins account!"

But what about sharing bad news or trying to persuade someone? Blurting it out won't work. Instead, lead up to your main point with background information or good reasons: "Even with all your hard work, we lost the account."

In short, the organization of each message should match your purpose—what you are trying to achieve. This chapter will help you organize with purpose.

Your Goal

Organize to present good news, bad news, and persuasive messages.

- Use the SEA formula for most messages.
- Use the BEBE formula to break bad news.
- Use the AIDA formula to persuade.

How should I organize most messages?

If your reader is likely to respond to your message as good or neutral news, be direct. Use the **SEA** organization formula: **S**ituation + **E**xplanation + **A**ction.

Situation
Explanation
Action

New Message

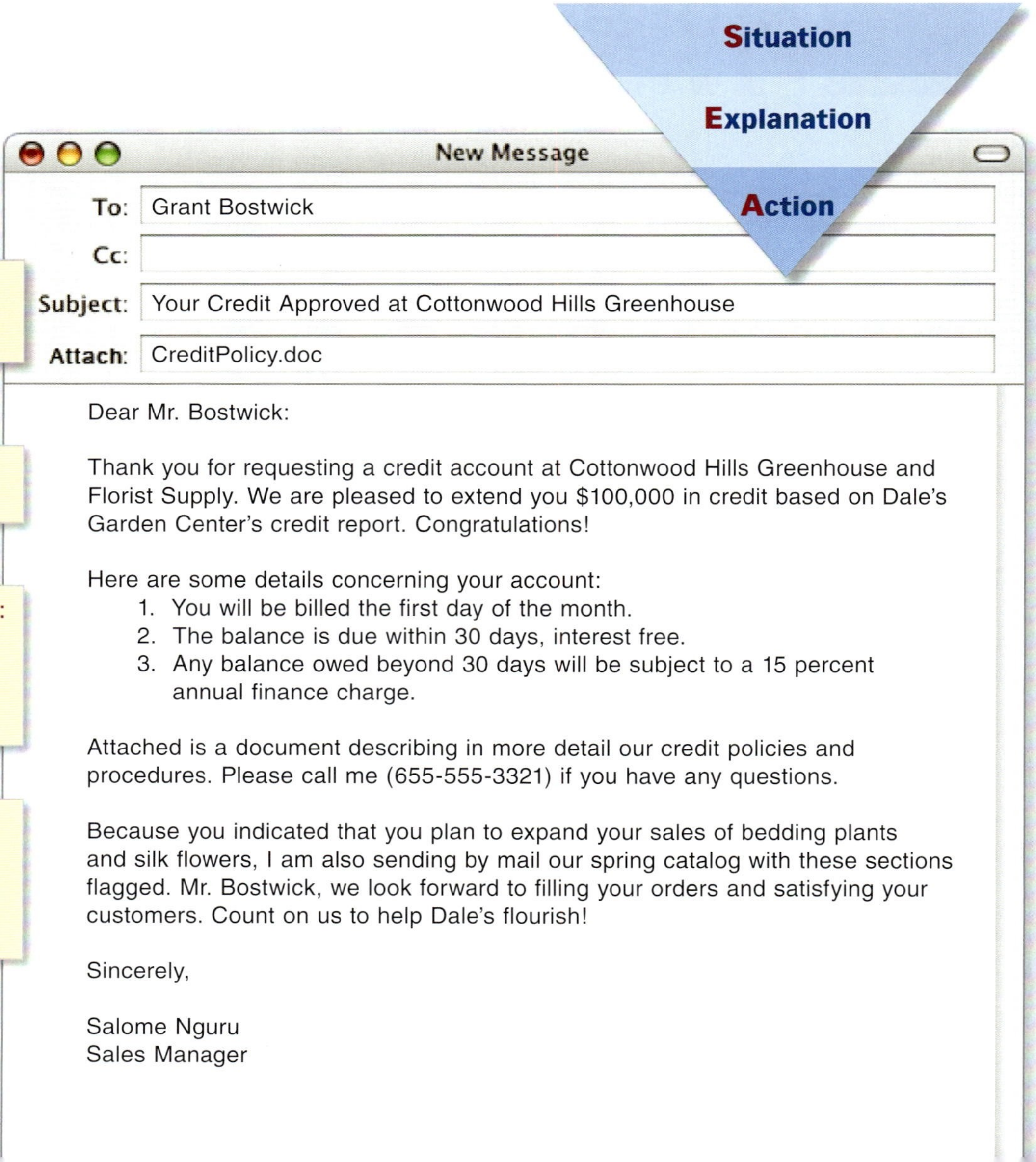

To: Grant Bostwick
Cc:
Subject: Your Credit Approved at Cottonwood Hills Greenhouse
Attach: CreditPolicy.doc

Dear Mr. Bostwick:

Thank you for requesting a credit account at Cottonwood Hills Greenhouse and Florist Supply. We are pleased to extend you $100,000 in credit based on Dale's Garden Center's credit report. Congratulations!

Here are some details concerning your account:
1. You will be billed the first day of the month.
2. The balance is due within 30 days, interest free.
3. Any balance owed beyond 30 days will be subject to a 15 percent annual finance charge.

Attached is a document describing in more detail our credit policies and procedures. Please call me (655-555-3321) if you have any questions.

Because you indicated that you plan to expand your sales of bedding plants and silk flowers, I am also sending by mail our spring catalog with these sections flagged. Mr. Bostwick, we look forward to filling your orders and satisfying your customers. Count on us to help Dale's flourish!

Sincerely,

Salome Nguru
Sales Manager

Situation: Write a clear subject line.

State the good news.

Explanation: Provide specifics of the good news.

Action: Focus on next steps and the future relationship.

Q How should I organize bad-news messages?

If your reader will likely be unhappy or angry with your message, be indirect. Use the **BEBE** formula: **B**uffer + **E**xplanation and **B**ad News + **E**xit.

Buffer

Explanation and Bad News

Exit

MEMORANDUM

Date: July 20, 2008
To: All Staff
From: Lawrence Durante, President
Subject: Recent FDA Plant Inspection

Use a neutral subject line.

As you know, this past Monday, July 18, the FDA came to our plant for a spot inspection. I'm writing to share the inspection results and our response.

Buffer: State your reason for writing.

The good news is that the FDA inspectors did not find problems warranting a shutdown of Premium Meats. The bad news is that the inspectors cited us for three major violations resulting in a fine of $90,000.

Explanation and Bad News: State the case factually and calmly.

Tell what has been done and what needs to be done.

The FDA is sending us a clear message. We must take immediate steps to protect our customers, our jobs, and our company. To that end, I have taken the following steps:

1. The Executive Committee met with me to review the FDA report and determine the problem areas in our production process.
2. I have directed the Production Management Team to review quality-control procedures and conduct two retraining sessions immediately.
3. I have appointed a Quality Task Force of both management and production staff to study the production process and make further recommendations.

Exit: Conclude positively but realistically.

If you have suggestions or questions, please speak to your immediate supervisor. Together, we can correct these problems.

How should I organize persuasive messages?

When your reader may be indifferent or even resistant to your message, be indirect. Use the **AIDA** formula: **A**ttention + **I**nterest and **D**esire + **A**ction.

Attention
Interest and Desire
Action

DAVISTOWN ARTS COUNCIL
340 South Edwards, Davistown, PA 15349 • FAX (724) 555-1438 • davistownac.org

March 15, 2008

Ms. Judy Niles
Brewster's Brew Coffee Shop
231 East State
Davistown, PA 15349

Dear Ms. Niles:

Attention: Hook the reader.

When folks want delicious coffee and scones, they think of Brewster's Brew. When they want great live music, they could also think of Brewster's. Read on.

Interest and Desire: Persuade the reader by focusing on benefits.

The Davistown Arts Council is launching Music Alive—a network of local restaurants that feature live performances. The musicians include singer-songwriters, classical guitarists, hammer-dulcimer players, a recorder quartet, and even a harpist. Your business would be a perfect venue for these performers.

Action: Ask the reader to take a reasonable next step.

Enroll in Music Alive today. Simply fill out the enclosed form, indicating your music-style preferences and the times you could host performers. We look forward to having you in Music Alive!

Yours truly,

Patrick Edstrom

Patrick Edstrom
President, DAC

Enclosure: Music Alive form

6 Writing Sales Correspondence

The difference between a warehouse full of inventory and an in-box full of orders may be a well-written sales message. A sales message must deliver a persuasive, logical, and trustworthy pitch.

- **A persuasive pitch** targets a reader's specific need.
- **A logical pitch** stakes a claim and provides strong support for it.
- **A trustworthy pitch** is based on facts and a solid business reputation.

This chapter will help you write sales messages that empty your warehouse and fill your in-box with orders.

Your Goal

Understand the basics of sales correspondence.

- Target your reader's needs.
- Make persuasive claims.
- Support your claims convincingly.
- Gain your reader's trust.

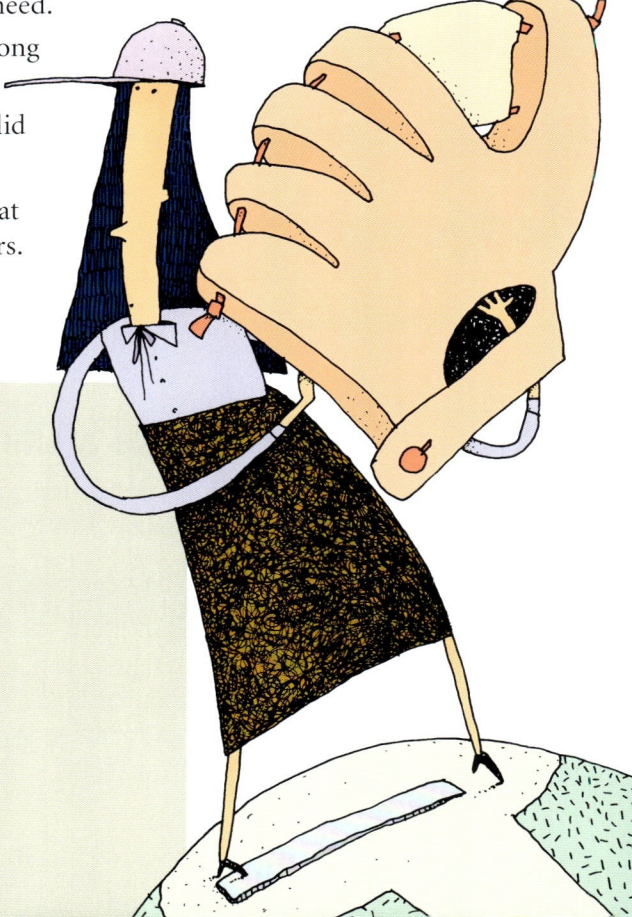

Q How can I target the reader's needs?

You can target a reader's needs by deciding exactly how your product, service, idea, or proposal fills those needs. In 1943, the psychologist Abraham Maslow proposed that all human needs can be represented in a five-tiered pyramid. The higher needs are important only after the lower needs are satisfied. Find the reader's need on the hierarchy and target it in your sales letter.

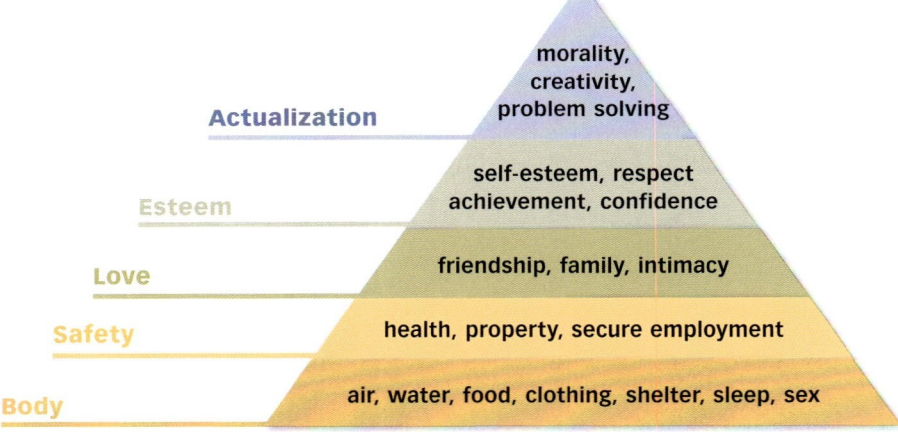

Q How should I make a claim?

State your sales claim by connecting your product, service, project, or idea with the need that it fulfills. Follow this formula.

Your product, service, project, or idea	+ The need that is fulfilled	= A strong claim statement
Earth-Scape's natural, sustainable landscape	easy to maintain, good for the environment, and inexpensive	Earth-Scape's natural, sustainable landscape is easy on your back, your backyard, and your bank account.

How can I test my claim?

Once you have made a claim, test it to make sure the claim is clear. Ask yourself the following questions:

___ Does my claim **focus** on the reader's needs and benefits?
___ Is my claim **specific**?
___ Can I **support** my claim with evidence?
___ Can I **persuade** my reader to care?
___ Can I **demonstrate** my reliability to make the claim?

How should I support my claim?

You should support a claim using provable facts that are . . .

- **accurate**—each detail is correct, not vague or confusing.
- **complete**—full, pertinent information is provided.
- **concrete**—general statements are clarified with specific details.
- **focused**—all the information relates to the stated claim.

Poor Support	Strong Support
Greenworld Sanitation is a favorite waste-removal company in Bloomington.	Greenworld Sanitation handles 75 percent of all business waste-removal needs in Bloomington.

What persuasive words should I use?

Persuasive words focus on the ideas, concepts, and values that the reader cares about. In addition to using the reader's name, use words like these:

you	endorsed	money	solution	supported
please	discover	tested	benefit	offer
thank you	ease	new	value	reduce
postage-paid	guarantee	proven	increase	privilege
appreciate	health	results	growth	credit
complimentary	love	save	approved	discount

Q How can I convince my reader?

Make sure that your support answers the reader's three main questions about the claim you have made, as in the following example:

QUESTION	ANSWER
1. WHAT DO YOU MEAN?	ANSWER WITH CLARIFYING DATA.
2. CAN YOU PROVE IT?	ANSWER WITH SUPPORTING DETAILS.
3. WHY SHOULD I CARE?	ANSWER WITH COSTS AND BENEFITS.

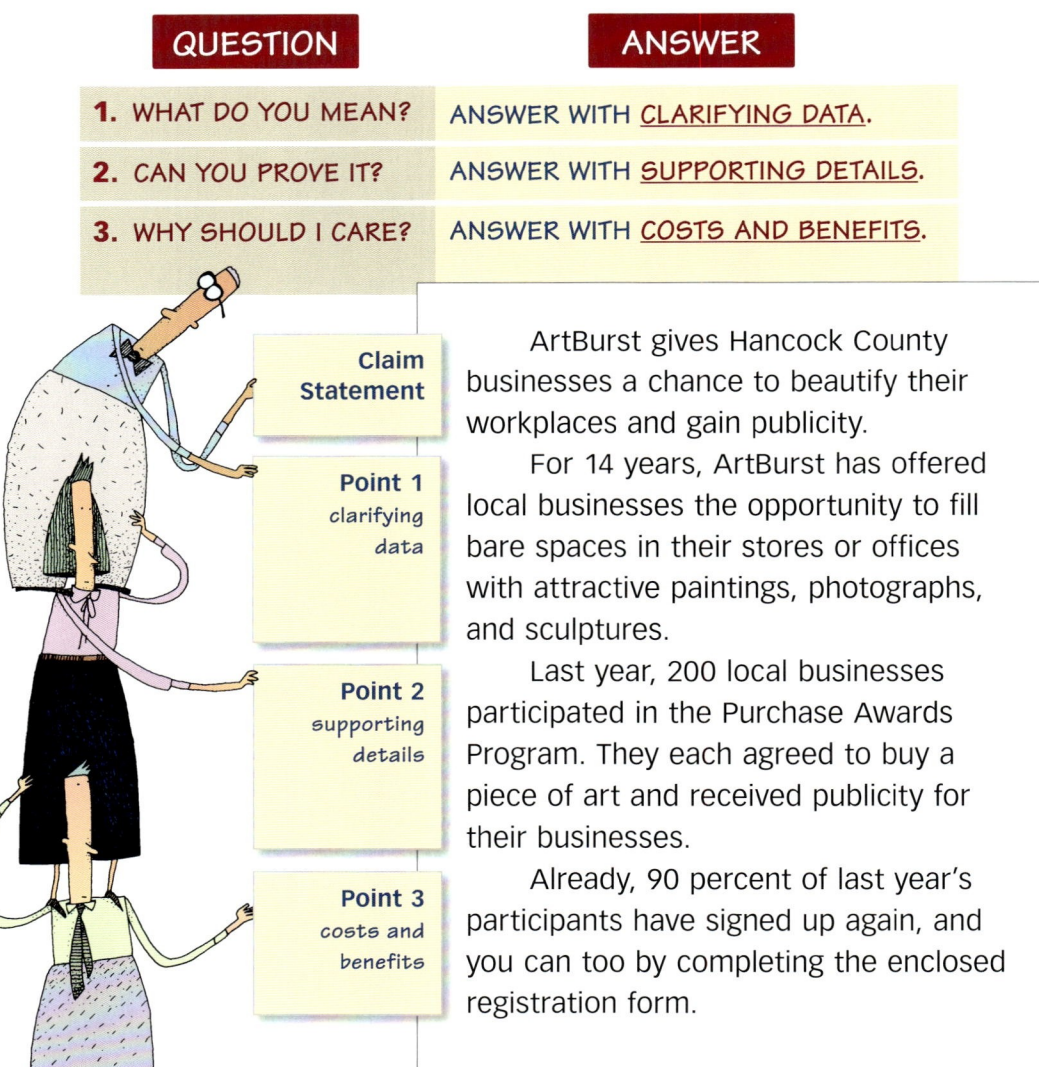

Claim Statement

ArtBurst gives Hancock County businesses a chance to beautify their workplaces and gain publicity.

Point 1 *clarifying data*

For 14 years, ArtBurst has offered local businesses the opportunity to fill bare spaces in their stores or offices with attractive paintings, photographs, and sculptures.

Point 2 *supporting details*

Last year, 200 local businesses participated in the Purchase Awards Program. They each agreed to buy a piece of art and received publicity for their businesses.

Point 3 *costs and benefits*

Already, 90 percent of last year's participants have signed up again, and you can too by completing the enclosed registration form.

How do I address competing claims?

Deal with your competition by focusing on the issue, making concessions, and developing rebuttals.

1. **Focus on the issue** and avoid negative talk. Instead of running down the competition, demonstrate the value of your claim.

Poor	Companies that provide dial-up services don't belong in the 21st century.
Better	Fat Cat Broadband brings the 21st century right to your desktop, laptop, or palmtop.

2. **Make concessions** to recognize the worthiness of the competition. Use words such as these:

admittedly	I agree that	of course
granted	I concede that	perhaps
I accept that	it is true that	you're right

Example	Admittedly, Fat Cat Broadband costs a dollar more per day than your dial-up service, but isn't your time and sanity worth that much?

3. **Develop rebuttals** that tactfully demonstrate an oversight or a flaw in the competition's argument. Here are three strategies:
   - **Reinterpret** the evidence.
   - **Provide newer, stronger evidence.**
   - **Stress the benefits** of your claim.

Example	Though dial-up services cost less, they also deliver less. Increasingly, Internet music, movies, games, and downloads require a broadband connection. Call Fat Cat to get the full Internet—at up to 10 times the speed.

TIP Concessions and rebuttals offer one more type of support for your claim. They show your knowledge of the competition and even allow you to use the competition's arguments against them.

How can I win the reader's trust?

Follow these tips to create a sales letter that the reader will trust:

- **Use facts.** Base your claim on verifiable facts instead of opinions. Avoid emotionally charged appeals.
- **Be honest and accurate.** Don't give false data, spin information, or ignore facts. Don't promise more than you can deliver.
- **Offer your credentials.** Experience, training, and history count for a lot. When appropriate, reference credentials such as these.

past projects	client lists	awards	endorsements
certification	education	reviews	memberships

- **Follow standards.** Send correct letters that adhere to your company standards and that use standard English. Also show respect for the reader's values, societal codes, and government regulations.

 How can I avoid verbal abuses?

Don't send angry messages. Also eliminate the following abuses, which show disrespect for your reader and others and may result in dire consequences.

The Seven Deadly Sins of Sales Letters

1. **Snipping, Sniping, and Snapping:** Don't nag, criticize, or show anger.
2. **Slamming:** Don't write derogatory comments.
3. **Defaming:** Never attack a person's reputation. (Libel is printed defamation, slander is spoken defamation, and both are grounds for legal action.)
4. **Swearing:** Do not use profane or vulgar language.
5. **Discriminating:** Never label a group or person based on stereotypes about race, ethnicity, gender, sexual orientation, or religion.
6. **Harassing:** Never use innuendos or manipulation.
7. **Threatening:** Do not tell readers they must comply or they "will be sorry."

7 Writing Sales Letters

Every business must do three things to survive: (1) **get the job**, (2) **do the job**, and (3) **get paid for the job**. One of your most powerful tools for accomplishing the first task is the sales letter.

This chapter explains how to write five types of sales letters:

- **Form letter**
- **Targeted sales letter**
- **Sales letter following a contact**
- **Sales letter following a sale**
- **Sales letter to an inactive customer**

Using this chapter's instructions and models will help you get and keep customers!

Your Goal

Create sales letters that get the job done.

- Use the writing process to hone your message.
- Write an opening that grabs the reader's attention.
- Build interest and desire.
- End with an effective call to action.

Q How can the writing process shape sales letters?

Follow the steps below to communicate your sales message efficiently and effectively.

1. Prewrite
Analyze your purpose, the audience, and the context.
- *What do I want the sales message to accomplish?*
- *Who is my reader? What does he or she need?*
- *How does my product or service meet that need?*
- *Who are my competitors, and what do they offer?*

Gather and organize details.
- *What qualities of my product will the reader recognize and value?*
- *What qualities must I explain or prove? How?*

2. Draft
Use a correct letter format and the AIDA formula.
- **Write an opening** that captures your reader's **attention**.
- **Develop a middle** that builds **interest** and **desire**.
- **Create a closing** with a call to **action** (who should do what, when).

3. Revise
Review the letter's ideas, organization, and voice.
- *Have I included all the information the reader needs?*
- *Did I organize my message using the AIDA formula?*
- *Do I maintain a conversational, professional tone throughout?*

4. Refine
Check your letter's words, sentences, correctness, and design.
- *Do my words have the right connotation (emotion)?*
- *Are my sentences clear, complete, and smooth?*
- *Is my grammar, punctuation, capitalization, and spelling correct?*
- *Are all names, dates, and details current and correct?*
- *Did I use a standard letter format?* (28–33)

FORM SALES LETTER

Dale's Garden Center
484 Leeward Avenue SE, Tuscaloosa, AL 35406-3770
Phone 908/555-8900, FAX 908/555-1600, E-Mail dalesgardencenter.com

February 1, 2008

Opening
Attention: Use a question or a similar strategy.

Dear Leighmaster College Student:

Have any of your science professors ever told you that plants can talk? Well, they can. Dale's flowers speak the language of love.

Middle
Interest and Desire: Tie features to benefits using vivid language.

If you're at a loss for words with Valentine's Day just two weeks away, let Dale's flowers help you. Red roses share your love in the traditional language of romance. A Southern Charm Bouquet containing the enchanting magnolia says it with class. Or choose our Valentine Special— "poetry" in a porcelain vase!

Closing
Action: Make action easy. Stress choices, value, and incentives. Restate your key selling point.

Check out the full-color selection guide enclosed, and then place your order by phoning 1-800-555-LEAF. If you call by February 13, we guarantee delivery of fresh flowers on Valentine's Day. Order by February 10, and you'll receive a 20 percent discount.

Let Dale's flowers help you start a great conversation!

Sincerely,

Jerilynn Bostwick

Jerilynn Bostwick
Sales Manager

Postscript: Explain a special benefit.

P.S. Is yours a long-distance romance? Remember, we deliver flowers anywhere in the world through the Teleflora network.

TARGETED SALES LETTER

605 CHERRY STREET   SIOUX FALLS, SOUTH DAKOTA 57103   (605) 555-2402

April 27, 2008

Mr. Andrew Larson
Larson and Kilgrew Wholesale Plumbing
1009 Walker Avenue
Omaha, Nebraska 68154

Dear Mr. Larson:

Opening — Attention: Create a catchy context for your message.

Last week I visited with Agnes Lead, Superintendent of Clark Elementary School in Vermillion, South Dakota. She and I discussed the parking-lot pavement project that Asphalt Specialists will do for her school in July.

Middle — Interest and Desire: Link the context to the reader's need and offer to address it. Present your key selling point.

At one point during that conversation, Agnes mentioned that you and she are cousins. She also said that you own Larson and Kilgrew Wholesale Plumbing, and that you might be interested in repairing a parking lot in front of your property and a private street that runs beside it.

I'm writing first to let you know that during August, Asphalt Specialists will be in your area to do two paving projects in southern Omaha. Second, I'd like you to consider having our company do your repair work. Because our equipment and crews will be in your area, we could offer you our quality work at a very competitive price.

Closing — Action: Describe specific follow-up action and close politely.

Next week I'll call your office to see if I might review your projects with you and give you a bid for their repair.

Sincerely,

Al Lempke

Al Lempke

SALES LETTER FOLLOWING A CONTACT

Rankin Technologies
401 South Manheim Road ❖ Albany, NY 12236 ❖ Phone 708.555.1980 ❖ Fax 708.555.0056

April 12, 2008

Mr. Henry Danburn, Manager
Titan Industrial Construction, Inc.
P.O. Box 2112
Phoenix, AZ 85009-3887

Dear Mr. Danburn:

Opening
Attention: Mention previous positive contact.

Thank you for meeting with me last week at the national convention in Las Vegas. I want to follow up on our discussion of ways that Rankin Technologies could work with Titan Industrial Construction.

Middle
Interest and Desire: Provide details the reader needs.
Build credibility.

Enclosed is the information that you requested: Rankin's corporate brochure, past and current job lists, recommendation letters, and more. I believe this material demonstrates that Rankin Technologies would be a solid match for your projects in western Illinois.

You mentioned that you will be the construction manager for the Arrow Mills renovation project in California. Rankin did the electrical installation on that project initially, and we would be very interested in working with you on the renovation. Someone who is familiar with our work at Arrow Mills is Mitch Knowlan, Plant Manager. He can be reached at 606-555-6328 or at mknowlan@arrowmills.com.

Closing
Action: Stress cooperation and the key selling point.

Henry, here at Rankin, we're excited about the possibility of working with you on any future project, the Arrow Mills project in particular. Please call me with any questions (507-555-9011).

Sincerely,

James Gabriel

James Gabriel
Vice President

Enclosures 5

SALES LETTER FOLLOWING A SALE

Dale's Garden Center
484 Leeward Avenue SE, Tuscaloosa, AL 35406-3770
Phone 908/555-8900, FAX 908/555-1600, E-Mail dalesgardencenter.com

December 6, 2008

Ms. Taryn Dionne
93 Claremont Crescent
Tuscaloosa, AL 35401-1553

Dear Ms. Dionne:

Opening — Attention: Thank the reader for previous business.

Thank you for your recent order of a Southern Charm Bouquet. We hope you were pleased with the arrangement.

Middle — Interest and Desire: Introduce other products without high-pressure tactics. Stress value and benefits.

Because this was your first order with Dale's, we're sending you the enclosed *2008 Occasions Diary* as a gift. The diary will help you remember important events in the lives of people you care about. You'll find room for birthdays, anniversaries, graduations, and more.

Flowers are a thoughtful gift for any occasion. That's why we've listed appropriate arrangements at the back of your diary. On the first page of each month, you'll also notice our monthly specials at the low price of $29.95 (plus delivery and tax).

Closing — Action: invite action.

So keep your *2008 Occasions Diary* handy throughout the year. Then just call our toll-free number on the inside front cover (or visit our Web site), and we'll gladly make all the arrangements!

Best wishes,

Bryce Calahan

Bryce Calahan
Customer-Service Manager

Postscript — Emphasize a special offer.

P.S. I've also enclosed a *Christmas Floral Selection Guide* filled with gift-giving ideas for friends and family.

SALES LETTER TO AN INACTIVE CUSTOMER

VERDANT LANDSCAPING
1500 West Ridge Avenue • Tacoma, WA 98466
564/980-1725

March 5, 2008

Ms. Karen Bledsoe
Blixen Furniture
1430 North Bel Air Drive
Tacoma, WA 98466-6970

Dear Ms. Bledsoe:

Opening
Attention: Express concern.

We miss you! While reviewing contract renewals, I noticed that Verdant Landscaping has not been scheduled to care for your grounds since the fall of 2005. You were a valued customer. Did our service fall short in some way? Whatever the problem, we want to try to serve you better.

Middle
Interest and Desire: Explore reasons for lost business and cite improvements.

During the past year, Verdant has expanded its services to help clients enhance the appearance of their businesses. A landscape architect is now available for consultations about improving your grounds. A tree surgeon is on call to care for trees and shrubs. Finally, our lawn crews now offer regular cutting with grass pickup or mulching. As always, we offer all our services at competitive rates!

Closing
Action: Encourage a first step and promise follow-up.

I'll call you next week to discuss whatever concerns you may have, and to offer you a 10 percent discount on your first month of lawn care. At that time, I can answer any questions you may have about our new services as they are described in the enclosed brochure.

Sincerely,

Stephen Bates

Stephen Bates
Customer Service

Enclosure

Checklist for Sales Letters

Use the checklist below to benchmark and revise your sales letters.

___ **Ideas:** The message states the main point clearly and convincingly, uses accurate and compelling details, and connects with the reader's needs.

___ **Organization:** The message follows the **AIDA** formula (**A**ttention, **I**nterest, **D**esire, **A**ction). In particular, the message includes

- an <u>opening</u> that gains the reader's **attention**, identifies a benefit to the reader, and supplies the necessary context.
- a <u>middle</u> that develops **interest** and **desire**; establishes a need and shows how to meet it; uses clear, convincing evidence to "sell" the idea or product; and anticipates and answers objections.
- a <u>closing</u> that asks the reader to take **action** and offers an appropriate incentive.

___ **Voice:** The tone is direct, polite, and personal, demonstrating sensitivity to the reader's needs and concerns; the tone is not manipulative, apologetic, or aggressive.

___ **Words:** The phrasing includes precise nouns, vivid modifiers, and energetic verbs and avoids clichés, jargon, flowery phrases, and "business English."

___ **Sentences:** The lengths vary from short to medium, and transitions tie ideas together.

___ **Copy:** The message is free of grammar, spelling, punctuation, usage, and typing errors.

___ **Design:** The message uses page layout, white space, headings, numbers, bullets, color, graphics, and typestyle to make content attractive and accessible.

TIP Like good proposals, good sales letters deliver their messages in a measured, objective voice that inspires the reader's trust. To achieve that voice, focus on creating a "you attitude" and on solving the reader's problem—not closing a sale.

8 Writing Customer-Service Letters

Sales letters and customer-service letters are similar in that both help you build your business. However, the two are also different. In a nutshell, sales letters help you *get* customers, whereas customer-service letters help you *keep* customers.

This chapter includes guidelines and models for addressing five customer-service situations. In each situation, the writer offers help that adds value to the product or service sold.

Your Goal

Create letters that keep customers coming back.

- Use the writing process to craft your message.
- Know your purpose, audience, and context.
- Clearly state your reason for writing.
- Support your main idea with key details.

How can I create customer-service letters?

Use the writing process to craft your message.

1. Prewrite
Analyze the situation.
- *Who is the reader and what is his or her need?*
- *What is the nature or history of the need?*
- *What agreements, guarantees, or policies shape my message?*

Gather and organize details.
- *What is my main point?*
- *What details will help the reader understand my main point?*

2. Draft
Organize your message using the SEA, BEBE, or AIDA formulas.
(SEA—good news, BEBE—bad news, AIDA—persuasive messages)
- Use the organizational formula appropriate for your message.
- Develop well-organized, complete paragraphs linked by clear transitions.
- State the news in a positive, objective, and professional voice.
- Include details that help the reader understand and accept your main point.
- Clearly state the context and implications of bad-news or persuasive messages.

3. Revise
Review your letter's ideas, organization, and voice.
- *Is my main point clear and supported with relevant details?*
- *Does the organization fit the situation and help accomplish my purpose?*
- *Is my tone informed, objective, and genuine?*

4. Refine
Check your writing for words, sentences, conventions, and design.
- *Have I used clear wording, a "you" attitude, and the reader's name?*
- *Are my sentences smooth and conversational?*
- *Have I checked punctuation, capitalization, spelling, and grammar?*
- *Is the formatting attractive and correct?* (See page **33**.)

INVITATION

Rankin Technologies
401 South Manheim Road ❖ Albany, NY 12236 ❖ Phone 708.555.1980 ❖ Fax 708.555.0056

May 30, 2008

Ms. Lorraine Scott
Sales Representative
206 West Dundee Street
Chicago, IL 60614

Dear Lorraine:

> **Opening**
> State the invitation politely.

Welcome to the Sales Seminar! I hope that you will have a productive week. While you are here, please help us celebrate Rankin's 20th anniversary.

> **Middle**
> Provide the context.
>
> Give all necessary details of the event.

This year, we have a lot to celebrate. Our office expansion is finished, and sales grew by 16 percent. On Wednesday, June 6, we would like you to be our guest at the following events:

- An open house from 8:30 a.m. to 4:00 p.m. with hourly tours of the new office, engineering, and manufacturing facilities
- A ribbon-cutting ceremony at 4:00 p.m. on the west lawn, with refreshments served at 4:30 p.m.

> **Closing**
> Anticipate participation and offer help.

You are a big part of Rankin's success, Lorraine. I hope that you can take a break from your busy seminar schedule and join us. If you need directions, transportation, or other information, please speak with Rebecca Wright or call Matthew Nicolai at 555-1980, extension 4, or send him an e-mail at mnicolai@rnkn.com.

Sincerely,

Robert Hershey

Robert Hershey
Vice President of Sales
RH/svw

POSITIVE ADJUSTMENT

1400 NW Academy Drive  Atlanta, GA 30425
Phone 412/555-0900   Fax 412/555-0054

July 9, 2008

Mr. Jamaal Ellison
Southeast Electric
1976 Boulder Road, Suite 1214
Charlotte, NC 28216-1203

Dear Mr. Ellison:

Opening — Provide necessary background, apologize, and offer solutions.

Thank you for your patience and understanding as we investigated the malfunction of the ATV16 drives that you had installed for American Linc Company. I apologize for the inconvenience caused to both your company and American Linc. Below is a description of the problem, along with our solution.

Middle — Explain causes and solutions clearly in neutral language.

Problem: Serial-link failure. In response to your report on the malfunction, AC Drives sent a technician to American Linc Company. He determined the cause of the failure to be a defective voltage regulator in the serial-link box.

Solution: Our technician replaced the voltage regulator and apologized to Jean Snow, plant manager. This morning I wrote a letter to Ms. Snow in which I acknowledged that the problem was ours (not yours), and I apologized for the inconvenience.

Closing — Express appreciation and focus on future business.

Thanks again for alerting us to the problem. With your help, it was resolved promptly. I look forward to future business with Southeast Electric.

Yours sincerely,

Elaine Hoffman

Elaine Hoffman
Product Manager

POSITIVE REPLY TO AN INQUIRY

ASPEN STATE BANK
4554 Ridgemount Boulevard, Aspen, CO 81225-0064, PHONE 459-555-0098, FAX 459-555-5886
contact@aspenstatebank.com

February 22, 2008

Christine and Dale Shepherd
1026 11th Avenue, NE
Aspen, CO 81212-3219

Dear Christine and Dale:

Opening
State the reason for your response and your appreciation for the inquiry.

Thank you for your inquiry yesterday about financing your resort project. I enjoyed discussing your project and appreciated your frankness about your current loan with Boulder National Bank.

Middle
Provide the reader with the desired information and stress its value.

Although you commented that you will seek an extension of your loan from Boulder National, I have enclosed Aspen State Bank's commitment letter, subject to the terms we discussed. Perhaps you will consider our package. The following rates are available:

>   5-year fixed rate 5.500%
>   10-year fixed rate 5.875%
>   20-year fixed rate 6.375%

In case you do not proceed with the Boulder loan, this commitment will be good for 60 business days from today (February 22). If lower rates are available at closing, you will receive the benefit of that reduction.

Closing
Anticipate and invite future contact.

Thank you for your interest. I hope that your project goes well. If we can't work together on this project, please keep us in mind for future credit needs.

Yours sincerely,

Cara Harrison

Cara Harrison
Loan Officer

Enclosure: Commitment Letter

BID REJECTION

EVERSON CITY PLANNING AND DEVELOPMENT COMMITTEE
Everson City Council • Everson, WA 98247-2311 • 306/555-2134 • www.eversonpdc.org

February 12, 2008

Mr. Felix Grove
Sea-to-Mountain Landscapers
8900 Coast Road
Seattle, WA 98134-6508

Dear Mr. Grove:

SUBJECT: Bid 4459 Everson City Park

Opening — Buffer: Specify the bid and thank the bidder.

Thank you for your bid to design and develop Everson's eight-acre city park adjacent to Kingston Elementary School and the Nooksack River.

Middle — Highlight the reader's strengths objectively, but specify why another bid won.

Your bid was competitive for several of the criteria outlined in our original Request for Proposals (RFP). Your cost estimates, experience, and references were as strong as those from other bidders. However, Earth-Scape Design's overall plan tipped the bid in their favor. By including a variety of native plant species, Earth-Scape's natural, sustainable landscape will require less long-term care and create less stress on the Nooksack watershed. Because their plan contained a variety of plants, it also offered added educational value.

Closing — If appropriate, encourage bidding on future projects.

The Planning and Development Committee appreciates the work that you put into your proposal. We look forward to your interest in future Everson projects.

Yours sincerely,

Alice Potter

Alice Potter
Development Committee Chair

CLAIM DENIAL

1400 NW Academy Drive
Phone 412/555-0900

Atlanta, GA 30425
Fax 412/555-0054

June 15, 2008

Mr. Jamaal Ellison
Southeast Electric
1976 Boulder Road, Suite 1214
Charlotte, NC 28261-1203

Dear Mr. Ellison:

Opening
Buffer: Restate the problem and show concern.

We have finished investigating your concerns about the ATV16 drives that you installed for American Linc Company. We do understand that the drive and serial-link failures have inconvenienced both you and American Linc.

Middle
Use sound evidence and state the rejection clearly.

Offer helpful alternatives.

After testing the drives you returned, our line engineer determined that they failed because the temperatures in the cabinet exceeded the maximum operating temperature of the drives, leading to electronic-component failure. As noted in the ATV16 manual, the drive may malfunction under such conditions. For this reason, we cannot repair the drives without charge. We would be happy, however, to consider the following solutions:

1. We could remove the drive's plastic cover and install a stirring fan in the enclosure to moderate the temperature.

2. We could replace the ATV16 drives with the ATV18 model, a model more suitable for the machine you are using. (If you choose this option, we would give you a 15 percent discount on the ATV18s.)

Closing
Focus on the next step and on future business.

Please let me know how you would like to proceed. I look forward to hearing from you and to continuing our partnership.

Yours sincerely,

Elaine Hoffman

Elaine Hoffman
Product Manager

Checklist for Customer-Service Letters

Use the checklist below to benchmark and revise your customer-service letters.

___ **Ideas:** The message addresses the reader's need, states the news clearly and diplomatically, and includes all necessary supporting details.

___ **Organization:** The message follows the organizational pattern (SEA, BEBE, or AIDA) appropriate for the type of message (good news, bad news, persuasive).
- Paragraphs are complete, unified, and linked by clear transitions.
- Lists are organized logically, making reading easy.
- The opening, middle, and closing flow smoothly from one to the next.

___ **Voice:** The tone is informed, fair, and objective, showing concern for the reader's need and situation. If an apology is offered, the tone is genuine and frank. If a complimentary remedy is offered, the tone is gracious and professional.

___ **Words:** The phrasing includes strong nouns and verbs requiring few modifiers.
- The words are common and clear—no "business English," clichés, or slang.
- Forms of address are appropriate and correct.

___ **Sentences:** The sentences are complete, clear, correct, and varied.

___ **Copy:** The message includes no errors in grammar; punctuation; spelling; usage; capitalization; or use of numbers, titles, and names.

___ **Design:** The page design is attractive with an appropriate letterhead, white space, typeface, and letter format.

Tips for Customer-Service Letters

1. When drafting a customer-service letter, remember that your goal is to serve—not to be served. Use common, polite language that communicates this point.
2. When delivering a bad-news message, be natural and honest, avoiding disingenuous language such as manipulative appeals, fake apologies, or pious platitudes.

9 Writing Sales Proposals

A sales proposal is one step in a dialogue between potential customers and vendors. If the proposal is solicited (requested), the customer starts the dialogue, usually by publishing a Request for Proposals (RFP) that spells out a need. In response, vendors write proposals that explain how their products or services will meet this need.

If the proposal is unsolicited (not requested), the vendor starts the dialogue. The proposal identifies a need or problem for the potential customer, explains why it should be addressed, and shows how the vendor's product or service will solve the problem.

Your Goal
Create a proposal that meets a need and gets the job.

- ■ Use the writing process to craft the sales proposal.
- ■ Focus on the reader's need.
- ■ Organize the proposal logically and effectively.
- ■ Use business etiquette and letter format.

Q What steps will help me write proposals?

1. Prewrite
Consider your purpose, audience, and context.
- *What exactly am I convincing my reader to do?*
- *As a potential client, what does my reader need and value?*
- *Why might he or she be skeptical of my proposal?*

Study the need and your product or service.
- Review information about the need: past correspondence with the customer, other customer publications, related service records.
- *Solicited proposal:* Study the request for Proposals (RFP), noting what information the customer wants, in what form, and by what date.
- Identify the benefits: how your product or service meets the need, plus the cost and effectiveness of your proposal compared with the competition.

2. Draft
Organize your proposal *exactly* as requested in the RFP. If you have no RFP, or if it lacks organizational guidelines, follow the order below for brief proposals. (For long or complex proposals, go to <UpWritePress.com> for additional instruction and a model.)

Opening Explain your purpose for writing:
- *Solicited proposal:* The customer needs little convincing, so focus on showing that you understand the need and can meet it.
- *Unsolicited proposal:* Prove that the need is real and demands attention. If you fail to do so, the reader will ignore the document.
- Briefly identify the need, state its importance, explain your product or service, note when and how you can supply it, and list the cost.

Middle Flesh out your proposal:
- *Solicited proposal:* Cite the RFP title, reference number, publication title (e.g., Web site, newsletter, journal), and date.
- *Unsolicited proposal:* Explain how you learned about the need, possibly by citing past contacts or other links to the company.

Description of Product or Service
- In objective, convincing language, fully explain what the need is and how your product or service will meet it.
- List precisely what you will do: procedures performed, materials provided, or products installed. Use graphics to illustrate how products will look and function.
- Explain why your product or service is better than those of competitors. You might stress product design, longevity, efficiency, warranties, replacement costs, or on-site service.

Schedule or Plan Provide timelines showing how the work will proceed. Include starting and finishing times for phases within the project.

Budget List all product and service options, plus costs. Be sure that your data are complete, accurate, and transparent.

Statement of Responsibilities Remember that you're legally responsible to complete the project or provide the products exactly as stated, for the costs cited. Spell out the details.

Qualifications Refer to past projects and awards, illustrating that your company does good work—within the budget and on schedule.

Closing Summarize your proposal:
- Stress its benefits and urge the reader to approve it. Offer to provide additional information or discuss the proposal.

3. Revise
Review your draft's ideas, organization, and voice.
- *Have I effectively explained the need and my product or service?*
- *Have I followed the organization pattern shown in the RFP?*
- *Is my tone confident and objective without being aggressive?*

4. Refine
Check your writing for words, sentences, correctness, and design.
- *Have I used lists and headings in parallel form?*
- *Have I used correct punctuation, capitalization, spelling, and grammar?*
- *Have I used reader-friendly format, layout, typography, and graphics?*

UNSOLICITED SALES PROPOSAL

Juanita Guiverra, Computer Consultant

368 Palm Palace Boulevard
Miami, FL 33166-0064
Telephone: 313.555.0010
E-mail: jguiverra@cnsult.com

November 16, 2008

Mr. Alexander Bennitez
Nova Advertising
664 Helene Boulevard, Suite 200
Miami, FL 33135-0493

Dear Mr. Bennitez:

Opening — Show that you understand the reader's need.

Do you have numerous projects on hold because your staff is too busy? Consider getting your projects back on schedule by outsourcing.

My areas of expertise include the following:
- writing, editing, and keyboarding documents
- processing mailings from start to finish
- developing spreadsheets or flyers

Middle — Relate your services to the reader's needs. Focus on reader benefits. Sell your credibility, pointing to enclosures.

Outsourcing with me offers the following advantages:
- no long-term employment commitment
- satisfaction guaranteed (most reworking at no charge)

You can put my ten years of experience in the advertising business to work for you. The enclosed pamphlet describes my services, equipment, and rates. I have also enclosed samples of my work.

Closing — Call for a doable response.

Mr. Bennitez, I can help Nova Advertising complete its projects in a timely and professional manner. Please call me at 555-0010, and I'll be available for an interview at your convenience.

Sincerely,

Juanita Guiverra

Juanita Guiverra

Enclosures 4

Postscript — Offer an incentive.

P.S. As a new client, your first in-office consultation will be free.

RFP FOR A SMALL PROJECT

Study the RFP below and the bid submitted in response to it (73).

> **Request for Proposals 6324**
> June 30, 2008
>
> Millwood Pharmaceuticals is soliciting proposals for its waste removal and recycling needs. Your proposal should specify a monthly fee for these services:
> - One eight-cubic-yard container for refuse, serviced twice a week
> - One eight-cubic-yard container for cardboard, serviced once a week
>
> In addition, your proposal should address the following issues:
> - Price for additional pick-ups as needed by Milkwood Pharmaceuticals
> - Your policy for maintaining and placing containers
> - Your ability to dispose of harmful or hazardous materials in accordance with all state and federal regulations
>
> Mail your proposal (include your e-mail address) to the address below for arrival no later than July 26, 2008. By Friday, July 28, you will receive a response by e-mail.
>
> Agnes Grey
> Millwood Pharmaceuticals
> 2211 Green Valley Road
> Tallahassee, FL 32303-5122

Q How should I respond to an RFP?

Follow the guidelines on pages **68–69** and the tips below:
Study the RFP carefully, noting its stated need and its

- title, code number, and contact information;
- legal requirements and conditions;
- organization, key words, technical terms, and voice;
- proposal design specifications (from format to graphics);
- contact information, due date, and requested follow-up action.

Provide the information specified in the RFP in the format called for, including appropriate headings and technical terms.

SALES PROPOSAL FOLLOW-UP E-MAIL

After you have submitted a proposal, consider writing a follow-up letter or e-mail to (1) alert the reader that you sent the proposal, (2) show that you care about the reader's need, and (3) invite the reader to contact you for further information.

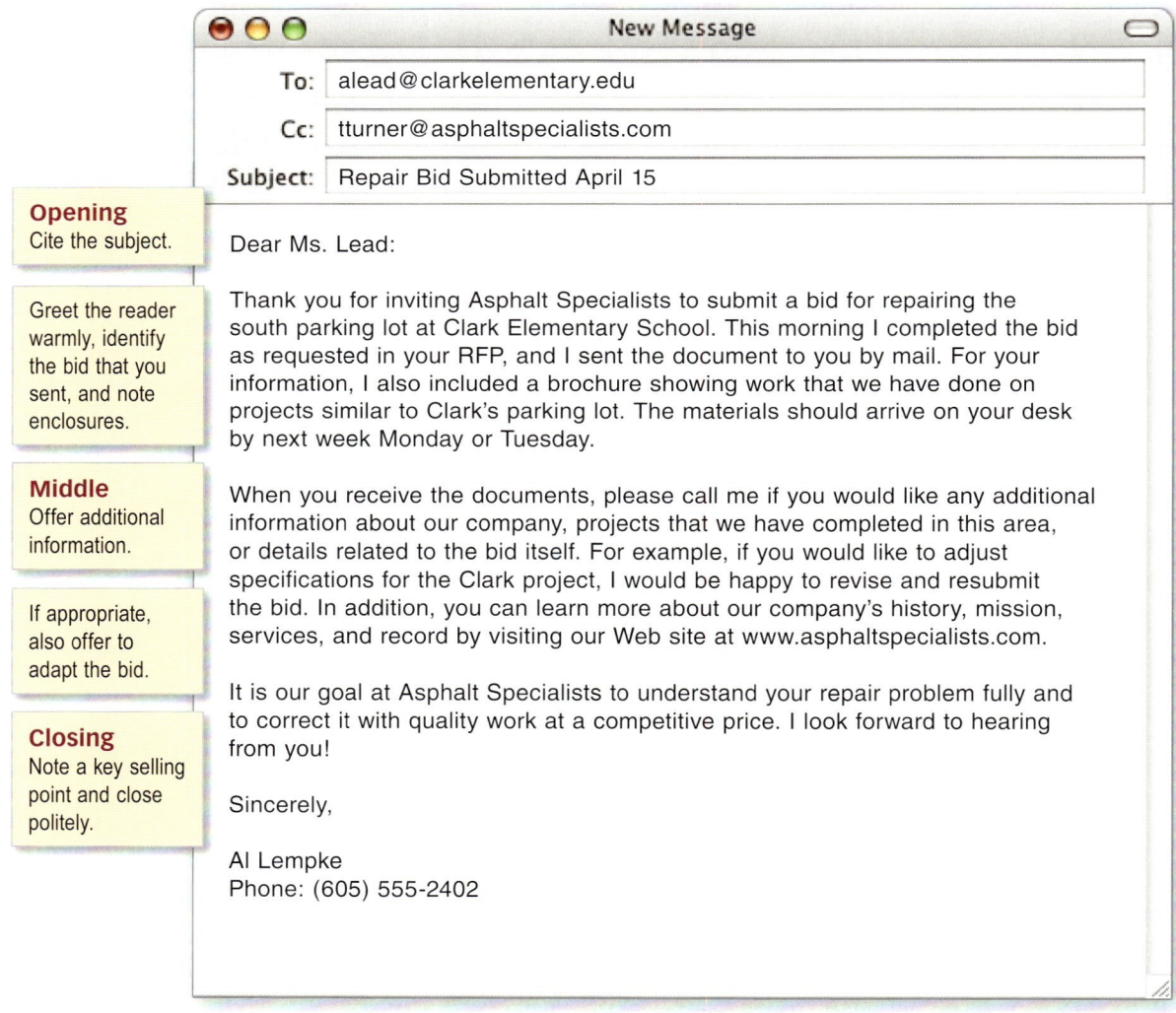

SOLICITED BID (USES THE RFP'S ORGANIZATION)

Note: This bid responds to the RFP on page 71.

 **BONIFACE SANITATION, INC.**
846 Watson Way   Tallahassee, FL 32308
302•555•2356   www.bonif.com

July 10, 2008

Ms. Agnes Grey
Millwood Pharmaceuticals
2211 Green Valley Road
Tallahassee, FL 32303-5122

Opening
Be positive and polite.

Dear Ms. Grey:

Thank you for the opportunity to bid on Millwood's waste-removal needs. We would be very pleased to take care of your refuse and recycling.

Middle
Reference the RFP. Use its organization and language to show that you understand its requirements and that your plan meets the need.

Sell your bid's value and your company's integrity.

Based on the bid requirements in your RFP 6324 (dated June 30, 2008), I am submitting the following proposal:
- One eight-cubic-yard container for refuse, serviced twice a week
- One eight-cubic-yard container for cardboard, serviced once a week
- Total cost per month: $169.00

If at any time your refuse volume proves heavier than anticipated, Boniface Sanitation will include extra pick-ups at $30.00 per trip. We also place the containers to suit your premises' appearance, use new or like-new containers, and empty containers at times you prefer. In addition, we can dispose of harmful or hazardous materials at competitive prices while meeting or exceeding all state and federal regulations.

Our goal is serving you well. As Tallahassee's leading waste collector, Boniface serves over 300 organizations like yours. I've attached references, crew lists, and equipment brochures for your review.

I look forward, Ms. Grey, to your response.

Closing
Anticipate a positive reply.

Sincerely,

Robert Estevez

Robert Estevez
Sales Representative

Enclosures 3

Checklist for Sales Proposals

Use the checklist below to benchmark and revise your sales proposals.

___ **Ideas:** The proposal
- shows a thorough understanding of the need, competitors' products or services, and your own product or service.
- offers a clear, persuasive line of thinking from beginning to end.
- contains accurate details, figures, and estimates.
- includes supporting graphics.

___ **Organization:** Solicited proposals follow the order stated in the RFP; unsolicited proposals follow the order spelled out in detail on pages **68–69**.

___ **Voice:** The tone is confident yet objective, showing concern for the reader's need.

___ **Words:** The language is readable; technical terms are defined as needed.

___ **Sentences:** Sentences read smoothly, are linked with logical transitions, and present information clearly.

___ **Copy:** The proposal contains no glaring grammar and spelling errors.

___ **Design:** Solicited proposals carefully follow the RFP instructions. Both solicited and unsolicited proposals use an attractive, accessible format.

TIP Like marketing documents such as sales letters, fliers, brochures, and ads, a sales proposal aims to persuade the reader that a product or service meets a need. However, the sales proposal is different in that it aims to persuade the reader about his or her specific need. The more that you know about your reader, the better tailored your proposal can be. To be convincing, a proposal must convey a thoughtful, objective voice, so the reader accepts it as a problem-solution document—not as an ad.

Section 3

Benchmarking Your Writing with the Seven Traits

In This Section

The following pages help you use the seven traits of effective writing to benchmark your correspondence.

Trait 1: Strong Ideas   78

Trait 2: Logical Organization   81

Trait 3: Professional Voice   85

Trait 4: Precise Words   89

Trait 5: Smooth Sentences   93

Trait 6: Correct Copy   97

Trait 7: Effective Design   101

10 Strengthening Seven Traits of Your Correspondence

All businesses must address quality control if they want their products and services to satisfy customers. Your business correspondence is no different: you need a quality-control system to make sure that your e-mails, memos, and letters accomplish your correspondence goals.

That's where the seven-traits benchmarks come in. You can measure your own documents' ideas, organization, voice, word choice, sentence smoothness, correctness, and design. But you can also use these traits as benchmarks for assessing others' writing and as a common vocabulary with which to discuss the quality of correspondence throughout your organization.

Your Goal

Employ the seven traits of effective writing.

- **Improve ideas, organization, and voice.**
- **Fine-tune words, sentences, and correctness.**
- **Create a reader-friendly design.**

Strong Ideas

TRAIT 1

At its core, correspondence involves exchanging ideas. To develop strong ideas, you need to make different types of claims, support them effectively, present them creatively, and treat competing ideas respectfully.

Q How can I strengthen my claims?

Use three different types of claims to achieve different goals.

1. A **claim of truth** argues about what is **correct**. It deals with facts. *Claims of truth should not be exaggerated, impossible to prove, harmful, or libelous.*

   > The Cubby Creator is the best-selling closet organizing system on the market.

2. A **claim of value** argues about what has **worth**. It deals with a known standard. *Claims of value should not be based on personal preference or emotional bias.*

   > The Cubby Creator sets up more easily, holds more clothes, and is sturdier than any other closet system in its price range.

3. A **claim of policy** argues about what should be **done**. The claim should be practical and desirable. *Claims of policy should not be simply wishful thinking.*

   > If you struggle with closet chaos, you need your own Cubby Creator.

Q How can I use different claims in AIDA?

As the examples above demonstrate, you can use the three types of claims in succession to build a persuasive argument in the AIDA pattern:

- Use a **claim of truth** to get the reader's . . . **ATTENTION**
- Use a **claim of value** to build . . . **INTEREST AND DESIRE**
- Use a **claim of policy** to call the reader to . . . **ACTION**

Back Your Ideas with Fitting Support

Your readers will accept your ideas—from a simple meeting reminder to a complex sales pitch—when you offer fitting types of support.

Q What kinds of support will fit my claim?

Select support based on what you want to prove or show to your readers.

To personalize a claim ⟶ use **observations and anecdotes.**

Zack Williams was failing first-year algebra before he started working with Middle School MatheManiac. Now Zack is tutoring his classmates.

To demonstrate an idea ⟶ use **illustrations and examples.**

Dental Associates can beautify your smile with tooth straightening, enamel whitening, and even porcelain veneers. See these before-and-after pictures.

To quantify a claim ⟶ use **numbers and statistics.**

Last year, 33,000 people attended the IndyCon Game Fair, and this year, preregistration is already 25 percent higher.

To authorize a claim ⟶ use **expert testimony.**

Consumer Reports rates Dan's Douser the best power washer in its class.

To forecast results ⟶ use **predictions.**

By switching from gas-powered lift trucks to electric lift trucks, Rankin Technologies will cut CO levels in its warehouse by 25 percent.

To examine an issue ⟶ use **analysis.**

Customers rate Candella Windows highly due to three factors: (1) energy savings, (2) ease of cleaning, (3) and quality custom construction.

To prove a claim ⟶ use **tests and experiments.**

The Firefly minivan earned a five-star safety rating from the National Safety Council.

Use Creative Comparisons

Consider using a strong comparison to deepen your ideas. Effective comparisons (as opposed to clichés—see **91**) are especially powerful in sales messages.

 How can comparisons improve my correspondence?

Comparisons can connect **unfamiliar** ideas with **familiar** ones.

Unfamiliar	⊕ Familiar
The K9 Automatic Vacuum cleans effortlessly.	The K9 Automatic Vacuum wanders your floors like a curious puppy, but instead of leaving hairs, it picks them up!

Avoid clichés: The K9 Automatic Vacuum cleans like magic.

Comparisons can make **flat** ideas **interesting**.

Flat	⊕ Interesting
Electronic banking is convenient.	With First National's online service, writing checks, adjusting accounts, or buying stocks is as easy as typing your name.

Avoid absurd comparisons: Make a hat your halo.

Comparisons can make **scattered** writing **unified**.

Scattered	⊕ Unified
Dan's Douser cleans thoroughly. The pressure quickly gets rid of even the driest material. Gentle jets brighten every surface.	Dan's Douser cleans like a *vigorous brush.* The pressure quickly *scrubs away* even the driest material but gently *polishes* every surface.

Avoid stretched metaphors: Dan's Douser works like an army in your hand. The jets are the soldiers invading Dirtland, and you are the general at the controls.

CAUTION: Do not mix metaphors. The results are confusing or silly: *While climate change worsens, most car manufacturers are sitting on their hands without a paddle.*

Logical Organization

Logical organization delivers your message in the most effective way. Create high-info headings, strong beginnings and endings, well-ordered paragraphs, and effective lists to help readers quickly grasp your message. Organize your correspondence with your busy readers in mind.

Q How do I write high-info headings?

Make sure your subject lines, titles, and headings help readers understand your message at a glance. Headings should serve as signs that guide the reader through the structure of your message. Follow these guidelines:

Use an effective pattern. Structure subject lines, titles, and headings by naming the topic and providing a specific focus.

Topic	recycling policy
Focus	office wastepaper
High-Info Heading	Policy on Recycling Office Wastepaper

Focus on precise and clear wording. Include key words that sum up the content. Avoid say-nothing words and confusing terminology.

Say-Nothing	Ideas	What Else?	The End
✚ Precise and Clear	New Procedure	Next Steps	Retirement
Confusing	Policy Objectives Re: PHAT System		
✚ Precise and Clear	Policy for Tracking Work Through Time Sheets		

Avoid phrases that "scream." Don't write headings in all capitals with multiple exclamation marks.

TIP Use parallel phrasing for headings. See page **95**.

Order Ideas in Paragraphs

Paragraphs structure your thinking into digestible "bites." A strong paragraph is a group of related sentences that develops a unit of thought and advances your main point. In addition, each paragraph performs a role in the message: introduction, support, or conclusion.

How can I strengthen the opening paragraph?

Make sure your opening paragraph does one or more of the following:

Create a connection.	Thanks for your bid on our office-space remodel.
State good news.	We accept the bid and want to begin construction.
Buffer bad news.	The bid-review team appreciates the careful thought that you invested in the proposal. However, it did not . . .
Begin to persuade.	*Business News* recently reported that poorly designed office space can reduce productivity by 25 percent and contribute to employee anxiety or depression.

How can I strengthen the closing paragraph?

Make sure the closing paragraph gives readers everything they need to understand your correspondence and act on it. Use one or more of the following tactics:

Summarize.	In short, we chose your design because it will improve our work flow.
Recommend.	While your bid was competitive on cost, it could support teamwork more fully.
Call to action.	Please sign and return the enclosed contract by May 1.
Anticipate the future.	I look forward to your completing this remodel.

Q How do I write strong body paragraphs?

Make sure that each paragraph begins with an effective topic sentence, includes supporting sentences, and ends with a concluding sentence.

The topic sentences should answer the reader's first question: *"What's your point?"* Check that your topic sentences follow this formula.

The main point of the paragraph	+	A specific aspect of the main point	=	An effective topic sentence
National Campaign for Literacy		works to help Americans learn to read		As you know, the National Campaign for Literacy has spent 14 years helping millions of Americans learn to read.

Supporting sentences should answer the reader's second question: *"Can you prove it?"* Check that your supporting sentences use facts, examples, and other types of details to develop the main point.

Examples demonstrate the point.	Through programs before and after school and special tutoring sessions for adults, our campaign has combated illiteracy in the U.S.
Statistics quantify the point.	For the past decade, the number of people we have served has typically grown by 5 percent per year—but last year, the number of clients grew by 15 percent.

The concluding sentence should answer the reader's final question: *"Why should I care?"* Check that your concluding sentence drives your point home.

> To meet this need, we plan to expand our campaign, adding 29 new programs, extending existing services, and asking for help from people like you.

TIP In each body paragraph, address only one main idea and develop it fully.

Present Information in Lists

Lists separate and order information, making points readable (easy to scan), memorable (easy to review), and actionable (easy to implement).

 How should I use lists?

Remember, first, to keep all items in any list parallel in structure (see page 95). Then follow these guidelines for developing and formatting lists.

Choose a fitting format for your list.

- **With a few items,** build the list into the paragraph. Use transition words like *first*, *second*, or use numbering/lettering, such as (1), (2) or (a), (b).
- **If you have many items,** each item is long, or you want to stress each—then place the items in a displayed list.

For a displayed list, arrange items sensibly and format the list correctly.

- **Introduce the list with a lead-in.** Generally, use a complete sentence that ends in a colon. With an incomplete sentence, drop the colon.
- **Use numbers to stress ranking,** sequence, priority, counting, or totals. Use bullets or other appropriate symbols to stress equality.
- **Align all items** within the list.
- **Indent list items 5 spaces maximum,** and align each item's second and subsequent lines under the first line.
- **If list items are complete sentences,** capitalize the first word of each and use end punctuation. If list items are fragments, generally keep first words lowercase and avoid end punctuation.

A Bulleted, Displayed List with Fragment Lead-In	A Numbered, Displayed List with Complete-Sentence Lead-In
My areas of expertise include ■ writing, editing, and keyboarding documents ■ processing mailings from start to finish ■ developing spreadsheets or flyers	Your high CO levels are a concern for three reasons: 1. High CO levels cause sickness and lower productivity. 2. Using summer exhaust fans in winter to reduce CO results in low humidity that damages wood. 3. High CO levels can result in a substantial OSHA fine.

TRAIT 3: Professional Voice

Readers detect more than words: they also hear tone and attitude. For this reason, use a professional, convincing voice—one that shows a "you attitude," communicates strength, and sounds natural.

Q How can I show a "you attitude"?

A "you attitude" focuses on the reader's needs, ideas, and feelings—connecting you with the reader and building goodwill. Do the following:

Use common courtesy. Start by asking, *"How does this topic and message impact my reader?"* Then show genuine concern with informative, polite phrasing.

	Blunt, Uncaring	The due date for departmental budgets is next Wednesday, and I have to have them on time. Put them in my mailbox.
⊕	**Polite, Informing**	Please note that the due date for departmental budgets is next Wednesday. When yours is ready, just place it in my mailbox. Thanks!

Pay attention to names. Spell names correctly and use proper courtesy titles. Include the reader's name at a key point or in the closing.

	Impersonal, Careless	This morning jim called from Midwest Electric to say that he needs bid specs on the lipco project. Better get it to him ASAP!
⊕	**Personal, Professional**	This morning Jim called from Midwest Electronics, asking for bid specifications for the Lipco project. Could you send them this afternoon, Tammy? Thanks!

Use personal pronouns positively. Use pronouns to focus on the reader when the news is good. Avoid pronouns and focus on the situation when the news is bad. Use *I*, *we*, *us*, or *our* to stress a team identity.

For Good News	Your sales presentation today was excellent!
For Bad News	Unfortunately, Wilson manufacturing didn't reorder.
For Team Identity	However, we did get the Johnson Inc. account!

Develop a Strong Voice

The most effective voice for business correspondence sounds knowledgeable, confident, sincere, and objective.

Q How can I sound knowledgeable?

Project your knowledge by showing understanding of the topic, the receiver, and the context:

Topic	Receiver	Context
■ Make a clear claim. ■ Use specific terms. ■ Provide evidence of your claim.	■ Ask, "What does the reader know?" ■ Ask, "What does the reader need to know?"	■ Acknowledge negative or competing factors. ■ Time your message to be effective.

Uninformed	We need something better for the warehouse due to the bad air.
⊕ **Knowledgeable**	By phasing out gas-powered lift trucks and phasing in electric ones, we could reduce CO levels in the warehouse to meet OSHA standards.

Q How can I sound confident?

Sound confident by cutting "waffle words" such as the following:

kind of	sort of	maybe	possibly	perhaps
I think	I wonder	I wish	a little	a bit

~~I wonder if~~ W̲e could ~~maybe~~ check with Lifter Inc to ~~kind of~~ see if they would ~~possibly~~ allow us to trade in our gas lift trucks.

If your writing sounds arrogant, you can create a confident voice by shifting the focus from yourself to the product, service, or idea that you are presenting.

Arrogant	I am Rankin's Salesperson of the Year because I alone recognize that our products are second to none.
⊕ **Confident**	Rankin produces high-quality products that I'd like to show you.

Q How can I show sincerity?

Again, the best way to show sincerity is to be sincere. If your writing sounds insincere, revise your work by following these guidelines:

	Eliminate sarcasm.	Your software request will be approved when you become CEO.
⊕	**Communicate directly**.	The software you requested is really appropriate only for managers.

	Remove flattery.	You are our most important customer!
⊕	**Communicate honestly**.	We value your business and want to make sure we are meeting your needs.

	Don't exaggerate.	Our microprocessors are the biggest revolution since the printing press.
⊕	**Communicate realistically**.	Our new microprocessors cut the calculation time of our previous processors in half.

Q How can I show objectivity?

Develop a thoughtful, objective voice by describing both your own products and competing products in measured, unbiased terms. Focus on provable facts, not on opinions or manipulation.

	Biased	Andersen Hardware offers the best paint and wall-covering products in St. Louis.
	Manipulative	If you care about your family, choose our products.
⊕	**Objective**	Andersen Hardware's Clear-Coat paint is guaranteed not to fade or peel for six years!

Use Appropriate Formality

The formality of your writing is similar to the formality of your business attire. A formal suit may be perfect for a meeting but not for a company picnic.

 How formal should my document be?

To hit the right tone, use the tips and table below.

1. **Consider your purpose.** What are you selling or proposing and why?
2. **Assess your readers.** How well do you know your readers? Are they inside or outside your organization? Did they request your proposal?
3. **Judge your topic.** How serious is the issue, need, or problem?
4. **Consider the form.** Are you writing a complex, formal document, such as a major client proposal, or a simple price quote to be sent as an e-mail?

Tone	Characteristics	Example
Formal *Use for* ■ Major letters/proposals ■ Messages to superiors ■ Messages to some people outside your company ■ Bad-news messages with legal implications	■ No contractions ■ Few personal pronouns ■ Serious tone ■ Objective style ■ Somewhat complex sentences ■ Specific (sometimes legal or technical) terms	The goal of Boniface Sanitation is serving the Tallahassee community. As indicated in the attached client list, Boniface contracts with 300 companies for waste removal.
Moderate *Use for* ■ Other letters or proposals ■ Messages to coworkers, equals, familiar people outside the organization	■ Occasional contractions ■ Liberal use of personal pronouns ■ Friendly but professional tone ■ Varied sentence structure	Our goal is to serve you well. As Tallahassee's leading waste collector, Boniface serves over 300 organizations like yours.
Informal *Use only for* ■ Personal notes *outside* the workplace	■ Frequent contractions ■ Free use of personal pronouns ■ Appropriate humor ■ Loose sentences ■ Jargon, slang, in-house word choice	Jimbo: Would you take a quick look at this bid and clean up the garbage—particularly any smelly punc. and grammar errors?

Precise Words

TRAIT 4

Effective correspondence requires precise nouns, vivid verbs, and careful use of technical terms. Fresh word choice also avoids flowery phrases, clichés, slang, and "business English."

Q What are precise nouns?

A precise noun names a specific person, place, thing, or idea. Compare the italicized nouns in the passages below.

Vague	In a few *weeks*, our *company* will have a *day* when *people* can come in and see all the *things* we're doing and *ideas* we're developing.	
⊕ **Precise**	On *March 28, Felton Engineering* will host an *open house* during which we'll display *samples* of our *products*, including *blueprints, sketches, models,* and *prototypes* of the *Flow-Thru Heating Unit*.	

General	equipment	employee	document
↓	welder	supervisor	order
Specific	Delcott PowerKeg 215	Supervisor Barnhardt	purchase order

Q What are vivid verbs?

Vivid verbs are action verbs that communicate clearly without the help of adverbs. Compare the italicized verbs in the passages below.

Bland	When that day *comes* up, everybody *should get* together, *be* real friendly, *talk* with everybody, and *give* them coffee and information.
⊕ **Vivid**	During the open house, the engineering staff *will welcome* guests, *offer* refreshments, *distribute* promotion packets, and *explain* our products.

Bland	put	clean	get
↓	arrange	wash	acquire
Vivid	decorate	scrub	buy

Use Correct Words

To present your message clearly, use correct words and appropriate nontechnical terms.

❓ How can I make my words clear?

Double-check the following types of terms: names, key words, homophones, numbers, and facts. Errors in these terms tend to be glaring.

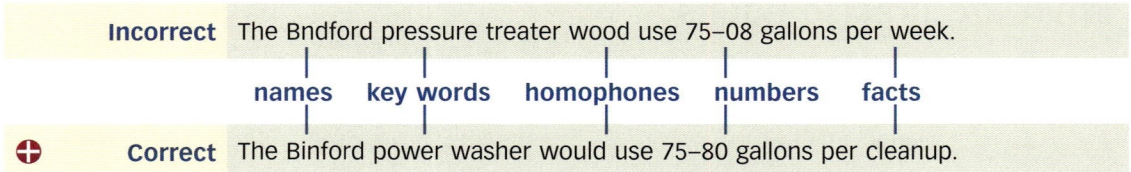

Incorrect	The Bndford pressure treater wood use 75–08 gallons per week.
Correct	The Binford power washer would use 75–80 gallons per cleanup.

(names, key words, homophones, numbers, facts)

❓ How can I use appropriate terms?

Be careful about how you use technical terms. Consider your audience and follow these guidelines when you write.

- **Use technical terms** when writing to a specialized audience.
- **Avoid technical terms** when writing to a general audience.
- **Define technical terms** when addressing a general audience.

Specialized Audience	Binford's Douser power washer delivers 2200 p.s.i., runs off standard a.c. lines, comes with 100 ft. h.d. synthetic-rubber tubing, and features variable pulsation options through three adjustable s.s. tips.
General Audience	Binford's Douser power washer has a pressure rating of 2,200 p.s.i. (pounds per square inch), runs off a common 220-volt electrical circuit, comes with 100 feet of hose, and includes three nozzles.

Replace Flowery Phrases and Clichés

In sales and proposal writing, tired terms generally show a lack of imagination and energy. Use more forceful, direct, and fresh language.

Q What is a flowery phrase?

Flowery phrases are words or groups of words that are unnecessarily fancy.

Flowery	With its broad-shouldered deck and powerhouse frame, the Sure-Built 226 is the atlas of utility trailers, able to muscle any load down any road.
✚ **Fresh**	The Sure-Built utility trailer has a solid 5′ x 12′ deck built with sturdy steel planks welded onto a 22 1/2″ x 3″ tubular steel frame.

Q What is a cliché?

A cliché is a phrase that has become tired from overuse. In many cases, the cliché was once a fresh metaphor or simile that no longer offers anything surprising. Writing dominated by clichés lacks originality and insight, so readers quickly tune out. (For more on creative comparisons, see page 80.)

> **FYI** Playing creatively with a cliché may revive its energy. For example, check this closing sentence in a sanitation company's waste-removal bid: "Until then, I'm at your 'disposal' to answer questions."

Clichéd	We are as good as dead if we *burn that bridge*.
✚ **Plain**	To meet our sales goals, we must accept the proposal.
Clichéd	We need *all hands on deck* because we have a *tough road ahead*.
✚ **Plain**	Everyone will need to work hard on the next project.

Some Common Clichés:

- as good as dead
- back to square one
- beat around the bush
- burn bridges
- can of worms
- easy as pie
- eyeball to eyeball
- go for broke
- last but not least
- movers and shakers
- pay through the nose
- piece of cake
- rear its ugly head
- rock the boat
- security blanket
- stick your neck out
- throw your weight around
- water under the bridge
- wet blanket
- work like a dog

Avoid Slang and Business English

Because neither slang terms nor business English is understood or appreciated by a broad audience, both should be avoided in sales correspondence.

Q What is slang?

Slang terms are casual, playful, and sometimes racy replacements for standard English. Because the words are often short lived and appeal to a narrow audience, they lack the power and clarity needed in business writing.

	Slang	The bucks we'd fork over for a primo power washer would pay off big time lickity split.
✚	Fitting	The savings realized by purchasing a power washer would pay for the washer in less than two months.

FYI An advertisement aimed at a particular group of people might effectively use slang to grab those readers' attention and speak in a voice they appreciate.

Q What is "business English?"

"Business English" is language that sounds stuffy, dated, or trendy. From pompous vocabulary that seeks to sound weighty and official to buzz words that fly through the air out of the most recent trend, what's the solution to such language? Plain English—the simpler and more basic the words, the better.

	Business English	The benchmark set is to maximize client pleasure by meeting demand with a supply of Southern hospitality. To facilitate maximization, management has upscaled your unit with no capital outlay required on your part.
✚	Plain English	Our goal is to provide you with outstanding service and warm, Southern hospitality. To that end, we have upgraded your room at no expense to you.

TIP Avoid business English terms like these:

| Applicable to | Attached hereto | Cognizant | Concur | Expedite | Operationalize |
| As per | Case in point | Commence | Endeavor | Heretofore | Wherewithall |

Smooth Sentences

TRAIT 5

In American football, an on-target pass enables the receiver to catch the ball easily and run with it. In correspondence, an on-target sentence helps the reader grasp the idea easily and use it. An on-target sentence is complete, smooth, and energetic.

Q What is a complete sentence?

A complete sentence has both a subject and a predicate that together deliver a complete, usable thought. For example, in the sentence below, *technology* is the subject—the sentence talks about technology. *Frustrates many people* is the complete predicate—it says something about the subject.

Technology frustrates many people.

In the examples below, the subjects are boldfaced. Notice that if you read only the subject or only the predicate, the sentence is incomplete and unusable.

Noun Subject	**Manufacturers** need technology to compete in a world market.
Pronoun Subject	**They** could not go far without it.
Phrase Subject	**To survive without technology** is difficult.

TIP Watch for subordinating conjunctions like those below. When they introduce a subject and predicate, the words that follow do not form a complete thought and must be joined to another complete sentence.

after, although, as, as if, as long, as though, because, before, if, in order that, provided that, since, so that, that, though, unless, until, when, where, whereas, while

Incomplete Thought	Although technology is transforming business
⊕ **Complete Thought and Complete Sentence**	Although technology is transforming business, technical training is not keeping pace.

Q How can I fix choppy sentences?

A series of sentences will sound choppy if they give all ideas equal treatment—rather than emphasize key points. You can fix this choppiness by combining and connecting sentences as shown below.

Combine by coordinating. Use coordinating conjunctions (such as *and, but, or, yet*) to join words, phrases, and sentences, showing equal relationships between ideas and details.

Choppy	The adjuster examined the roof. She checked the valleys closely. She also inspected the carport.
Smooth	The adjuster examined the roof, checked the valleys, and inspected the carport.

Combine by subordinating. Use a subordinating conjunction (such as *before, after, because, unless*) to place secondary details in a dependent clause or phrase (underlined below) and to place key points in the main clause (in italics below).

Choppy	I have done a lot of training in the health-care system. That includes more than 200 clients. My training experience spans seven years.
Smooth	During the last seven years, *I have trained more than 200 clients in the health-care system.*

Connect with transitions. Use linking words (in italics below) to create transitions that help form a series of logically related sentences.

Choppy	The starting date of August 24 works well for me. Thank you for the material you sent about moving costs and real-estate agencies. Could you please send information about area schools?
Smooth	*As we discussed earlier*, the starting date of August 24 works well for me. *In addition to* the material you've already provided about moving costs and real-estate agencies, please send information about area schools.

TIP When you combine choppy sentences, avoid creating long, rambling sentences. Rambling sentences connect many unrelated ideas and lack focus.

How does parallel structure improve sentences?

Parallel structure puts similar ideas in a similar grammatical form. This form (a) saves words, (b) shows that the ideas are related, and (c) creates a pleasing rhythm. Follow these guidelines:

LINK ideas in a list by using parallel words or phrases.

	Unparallel	I have instructed clients in Microsoft Windows, WordPerfect, not to mention my familiarity with Adobe InDesign.
⊕	Parallel	I have instructed clients in Microsoft Windows, WordPerfect, and Adobe InDesign.
	Unparallel	I have hospital experience developing job descriptions, have even been recruiting technical employees, and in the training of human-resources personnel.
⊕	Parallel	I have hospital experience developing job descriptions, recruiting technical employees, and training human-resources personnel.

TIP For more on lists, see page 84.

COMPARE ideas using parallel forms and coordinating conjunctions (and, but, or, nor, for, yet, so).

	Unparallel	Our hospital hires L.P.N. nurses, nurses with R.N. degrees, but also some B.S.N. nurses.
⊕	Parallel	Our hospital hires nurses with these certifications: Licensed Practical Nurse (L.P.N.), Registered Nurse (R.N.), and Bachelor of Science in Nursing (B.S.N.).

CONTRAST ideas using parallel forms and correlative conjunctions (either, or; neither, nor; not only, but also; as, so; whether, so; both, and).

Note: Be sure to include both parts of a correlative conjunction.

	Weak Contrast	Rankin turned 20 this year. It experienced 16 percent growth in sales also.
⊕	Strong Contrast	Rankin *not only* turned 20 this year *but also* experienced 16 percent growth in sales.

Q How can I energize my writing?

Avoid nominalizations, expletives, and passive voice, which can make writing sluggish and wordy.

A nominalization is a verb that has been turned into a noun. Find the verb in the nominalization and use it to revise your sentence.

Sluggish and Wordy	Energetic
I gave a **description** of the product.	I described the product.
I provided a **recommendation** for it.	I recommended it.

Expletives are filler words such as *it is* and *there is.* They serve no purpose in most sentences. Remove the expletive to energize the sentence.

Sluggish and Wordy	Energetic
It is certain we will finish on budget.	We certainly will finish on budget.
There is also our adherence to the deadline.	We also will adhere to the deadline.

Passive voice means the subject of the sentence is being acted upon rather than doing the action. Find what is doing the action and make it the subject.

Sluggish and Wordy	Energetic
The meeting **will be attended** by Paul.	Paul will attend the meeting.
A great time **was had** by everyone.	Everyone had a great time.

TIP Passive voice has some valuable uses. When delivering bad news or when the agent is unknown or unimportant, use passive voice to accent the result versus the doer.

Don't Write	Do Write
Jim turned down your request.	Your request has been turned down.
National Mutual has approved your loan.	Your loan has been approved.

Strengthening Seven Traits of Your Correspondence 97

TRAIT 6

Correct Copy

In correspondence, basic errors in grammar or mechanics imply that the writer is careless and unprofessional. To avoid this implication, edit your correspondence carefully before sending it.

Q What are the most common errors?

The errors listed below cause the most problems in business correspondence.

- Double subjects
- Double negatives
- Double prepositions
- Nonstandard substitution
- Unclear pronoun reference
- Pronoun-antecedent agreement
- Misplaced modifiers
- Dangling modifiers
- Squinting modifiers
- Subject-verb agreement

Q How can I avoid nonstandard constructions?

Below are four common errors that you should learn to identify and correct:

Double Subject	The design *staff, they* won't be happy with this decision.
⊕ **Correct**	The design *staff* won't be happy with this decision.
Double Negative	There *wasn't no* hint of trouble at the previous meeting.
⊕ **Correct**	There *was no* hint of trouble at the previous meeting.
Double Preposition	The engineering staff went *off to* the convention.
⊕ **Correct**	The engineering staff went *to* the convention.
Nonstandard Substitution	Jessica needs *to try and* get here on time. Except for her tardiness, she *would of had* a spotless work review.
⊕ **Correct**	Jessica needs *to* get here on time. Except for her tardiness, she *would have had* a spotless work review.

Use Correct, Clear Wording

Clear wording makes your writing understandable. To achieve this clarity, check for unclear pronoun references and errors in pronoun-antecedent agreement.

Q What is an unclear pronoun reference?

An unclear pronoun reference occurs when the reader is unsure what word the pronoun refers to, as in the examples below.

"Who," "which," and "that" clauses: Relative pronouns connect dependent clauses to the main clause. Like other pronouns, *who, which*, and *that* must refer to a specific noun or noun phrase. In addition, the relative pronoun should immediately follow the word (or words) it refers to.

	Unclear	Return the surveys by Monday, *which* will complete the review process.	***Which*** is unclear—it doesn't refer to a specific noun.
⊕	Clear	The *surveys, which* will complete the review process, should be returned by Monday.	

"It," "this," "that," and "they": These pronouns should refer to a specific noun. Don't use them to refer to an entire sentence.

	Unclear	The building includes a residence and a small coffee shop. Does *this* conform to zoning bylaws?	***This*** refers to the preceding sentence.
⊕	Clear	The building includes a residence and a small coffee shop. Does *multiple use* conform to zoning bylaws?	

Q What is pronoun-antecedent agreement?

Each pronoun must "agree with" its antecedent, meaning that both must be singular or both must be plural.

	Incorrect	*Everyone* is accepted, regardless of *their* skills.	***Everyone*** is singular; ***their*** is plural.
⊕	Correct	*Everyone* is accepted, regardless of *his* or *her* skills.	

Use Modifiers Clearly

To ensure that adjectives and adverbs are clear, avoid sentence structures in which these modifiers are misplaced, dangling, or squinting.

Q How do I avoid misplaced modifiers?

Misplaced modifiers are unclear because they are placed incorrectly. To fix the error, place a modifier as close as possible to what it modifies.

	Misplaced	Please review the pamphlet describing my services and equipment *enclosed*.	Does *enclosed* modify *equipment*?
✚	**Correct**	Please review the *enclosed* pamphlet describing my services and equipment.	*Enclosed* clearly modifies *pamphlet*.

Q How do I avoid dangling modifiers?

Dangling modifiers are unclear because the word being modified is missing or far removed. To fix the error, insert the necessary noun or pronoun, or change the dangling phrase into a clause.

	Dangling	*Having committed to meeting with us,* our regular attendance would be appreciated.	Who *committed to meeting with us*?
✚	**Correct**	*Having committed to meeting with us, Robert and Miriam* would appreciate our regular attendance.	Robert and Miriam *committed* . . .

Q How do I avoid squinting modifiers?

Squinting modifiers are unclear because they are located between two sentence parts, either of which the modifier could describe.

	Squinting	Any periodic reports that you have written *promptly* submit to Richard.	Does *promptly* modify *have written* or *submit*?
✚	**Clear**	*Promptly* submit to Richard any periodic reports that you have written.	

Make Sure Subjects and Verbs Agree

Each subject must "agree with" its verb: both singular or both plural.

Q How do I avoid subject-verb agreement errors?

Understand the four types of agreement errors.

First, disagreement can happen when words, phrases, or clauses separate a subject and verb, and the two disagree in number.

Incorrect	Each Homes Unlimited affiliate, as well as HU's worldwide partners, *depend* on volunteers.	***Affiliate*** is singular, but ***depend*** is plural.
⊕ Correct	Each Homes Unlimited *affiliate*, as well as HU's worldwide partners, *depends* on volunteers.	

Second, disagreement can happen when compound subjects joined by *and* need a plural verb, but a singular verb is used instead. With compound subjects joined by *or* or *nor*, the verb must agree with the nearer subject.

Incorrect	Local HU *affiliates* or the *director initiate* the partnership.	***Director*** is singular, but ***initiate*** is plural.
⊕ Correct	Local HU affiliates or the *director initiates* the partnership.	

Third, as subjects, singular indefinite pronouns take singular verbs, even when words come between them. Singular indefinite pronouns include the following: *each, either, neither, one, everyone, everybody, everything, someone, somebody, anybody, anything, nobody, another.*

Incorrect	*Everybody* in the divisions *contribute* 50 hours of labor.	***Everybody*** is singular; ***contribute*** is plural.
⊕ Correct	*Everybody* in the divisions *contributes* 50 hours of labor.	

Fourth, a collective noun, which names a group (committee, department, board), is singular when referring to the group and plural when referring to the members as individuals.

Incorrect	The local *committee check* the work schedule.	Acting as one body, ***committee*** is singular, but ***check*** is plural.
⊕ Correct	The local *committee checks* the work schedule.	

Effective Design

Quality design strengthens your correspondence by showing professionalism, helping readers find what they need, and making a response easy. Your document may have only seconds to get your message across, so make sure it is "dressed to impress."

Q What basic design principles should I follow?

1. **See readers reading.** Understand that readers . . .
   - are generally very busy and surrounded by distractions.
   - skim a document before reading closely.
   - may perform a task while reading.
   - read pages from left to right and top to bottom.
   - make sense of information both verbally and visually.
   - digest information in small chunks, not wholes.

2. **Make pages open and balanced.** Avoid lengthy passages of prose by effectively combining print and white space.

3. **Go with the flow.** Design pages so that information—both text and graphics—flows naturally from upper left to lower right.

4. **Develop consistent visual "cues."** Design elements should distinguish between main and secondary points, as well as show how the points connect or contrast with one another:
   - Information and ideas that are related should be clumped together, and their connections should be shown visually through similarities in size, shape, color, and alignment of material on the page.
   - Ideas that are contrasted should be signaled visually through differences in size, shape, location, and color of elements on the page.

Index

Message,
  Bad-news, 43. See also *bad-news messages*
  Context, 6
  E-mail, 16–18
  Good-news, 42. See also *good-news and neutral messages*
  Instant, 13, 14
  Medium, 5, 7
  Persuasive, 44. See also *persuasives messages*
  Receiver, 5, 6
  Sender, 5
  Written, 7
Misplaced modifiers, 99
MODELS,
  Addressed envelope, 39
  Announcement, 43
  Apology, 62
  Bid rejection, 64
  Claim denial, 65
  Cover sheet, fax, 24
  Credit approval, 42
  Crisis management memo, 43
  E-mail, 17
  Faxed message, 24
  Good-news announcement/notice, 42
  Information request, 15
  Inquiry reply, 29, 31
  Invitation, 61
  Letter,
    Basic, 29
    Expanded, 31
  Memo,
    Basic, 21
    Expanded, 23
  Negative announcement, 43
  Positive adjustment, 62
  Proposal rejection, 64
  Sales letter, 53–57
    First contact, 53
    Following a contact, 55
    Following a sale, 56
    Inactive customer, 57
    Targeted, 54
  Sales proposal,
    Follow-up, 72
    Letters, 70, 73

  Request (RFP), 71
  Thank-you message, 42, 72

Moderate tone, 88
Modifiers,
  Dangling, 99
  Misplaced, 99
  Squinting, 99

N

Negative announcement, 43
Negative language, 50
Neutral messages, 42
Nominalization, 96
Nonstandard language, 97
Noun,
  Collective, 100
  General, 89
  Precise, 89
  Specific, 89

O

Official titles, 36
Organization,
  According to purpose, 41–44
  Logical, writing trait, 81–84

P

Paragraphs,
  Body, 83
  Closing, 82
  Opening, 82
Parallelism, 95
Passive voice, 96
PERSUASIVE messages,
  Guidelines, 44
  Model, 44
  Sales letters,
    First contact, 53, 54
    Following a contact, 55
    Following a sale, 56
    Inactive customer, 57
Photographs, 104
Plain English, 92
Positive adjustment message, 62
Postal Service, U.S. envelope guidelines, 39

Postscript, 53, 56
Prewriting, 16, 20, 27, 52, 60, 68
Professional titles, 34
Pronoun,
  Indefinite, 100
  Personal, 85
  Relative, 98
  Unclear reference, 98
Pronoun-antecedent agreement, 98
  Plural pronouns, 98
  Singular pronouns, 98
PROPOSALS,
  Checklist, 74
  Follow-up E-mail, 72
  Guidelines, 68–69
  Rejection of, 64
  Request for proposals (RFP), 71
  Sales letter, 51–58
  Solicited bid, 71, 73
  Unsolicited, 70

R

Reference line, letter, 30
Refining, 16, 20, 27, 52, 60, 69
Rejections,
  Bid, 64
  Claim denial, 65
Relative pronouns, 98
Religious titles, 37
Reply to an inquiry, 29, 31
Revising, 16, 20, 27, 52, 60, 69

S

SALES letters, 45–58
  Avoiding verbal abuse, 50
  Checklist, 58
  Counter competing claims, 49
  First contact, 46, 53, 54
  Following a contact, 55
  Following a sale, 56
  Inactive customer, 57
  Support claims, 47–48
  Target needs, 46
  Trust, 50

Sales proposals, 67–74
    Checklist, 74
    Follow-up, 72
    Guidelines, 68–69
    Request for, 71
    Solicited, 73
    Unsolicited, 70
Salutation,
    Letter, 28, 34–37
    Punctuating, 28
SEA, 42
Semiblock letter format, 32–33

SENTENCE,
    Combining, 94
    Complete, 93
    Concluding, 83
    Supporting, 83
    Topic, 83

Sentence problems,
    Agreement, 100
    Choppy, 94
    Rambling, 94
Sentences, smooth, traits, 93–96
Signature block, 28, 30
Simplified letter format, 32–33
Situation analysis worksheet, 6
Slang, 92
Subject-verb agreement, 100
    Collective nouns, 100
    Compound subjects, 100
    Indefinite pronouns, 100
    Subjects with *or/nor*, 100
Subordinating conjunctions, 94

Technical words, 90
Thank-you message, 63, 73
Tips & techniques,
    Drafting, 16, 20, 27, 52, 60, 68
    Prewriting, 16, 20, 27, 52, 60, 68
    Refining, 16, 20, 27, 52, 60, 69
    Revising, 16, 20, 27, 52, 60, 69
Titles, forms of address, 34–37
    Capitalizing, 28
    Courtesy, 35
    Gender specific, 35
    Official, 36
    Professional, 34
    Religious, 37
Tone, 88
TRAITS of good writing,
    Clear words, 90, 98
        Fair, respectful language, 85
        Fresh, precise words, 89
        Wordiness, 91, 96
    Conversational voice,
        Natural, 85, 88
        Positive, 85, 88
        "You attitude," 85
    Correct copy, 97-100
        Faulty sentences, 99
        Nonstandard language, 97
        Unclear wording, 98
    Logical organization, 81
        Lists, use of, 84
        Three-part structure, 82–83
    Reader-friendly design,
        Format, 101
        Model, 102, 104
        Page layout, 102
        Typography, 103
    Smooth sentences, 93
        Choppy sentences, 94
        Rambling sentences, 94
        Use of transitions and linking words, 94, 95
    Strong ideas, 78–80

Transitions, 94
Transmitting notes, 30
Typestyles, 103
Typography, 103

Unclear wording, 98
Unparallel construction, 95
U.S. Postal Service envelope guidelines, 39

Verb,
    Passive vs. active, 96
    Vivid, 89
Verbal abuse,
    Avoiding, 50

Voice,
    Appropriate formality, 88
    Confident, 86
    Conversational, 85, 88
    Knowledgeable, 86
    Objectivity, 87
    Passive vs. active, 96
    Professional, traits, 85–88
    Sincerity, 87

White space,
    Using, 102

WORDING,
    Ambiguous, 98–99
    Creative comparisons, 80
    Dangling modifiers, 99
    Indefinite pronoun reference, 98
    Misplaced modifiers, 99
    Precise, 89–92
    Unclear wording, 98–99

Words,
    Clear and correct, 90
    Precise, writing trait, 89–92
    Technical, 90
    Transition, 44
    Waffle, 86
Worksheet,
    Situation analysis, 6
Writing sales letters, 51–58
    Checklist, 58
    Following a contact, 55
    Following a sale, 56
    Form letter, 53
    Guidelines, 52
    Inactive customer, 57
    Targeted, 54
Writing successful correspondence, 3–8